Dietrich

The Story of a Star

Dietrich

Leslie Frewin

STEIN AND DAY/*Publishers*/New York

In my research for this book I have been helped by many people—too
many to thank individually. But those of them who read this book
will know how useful their assistance has been and my thanks are
due to them all, particularly Michael Bateman. Among organisations
I must single out The British Film Institute, The Museum of
Modern Art, New York, the American Air Forces and MacGibbon
and Kee Limited for having been particularly courteous and
resourceful in helping me.

I acknowledge, too, permission to quote Mr Cecil Beaton from
his *Cecil Beaton's Scrapbook*, published by Batsford, in 1937.
Mr Beaton wishes it to be known that the quoted passage would not
represent his summation of Miss Dietrich as she is today.

LF

Printed in the United States of America

Stein and Day/*Publishers*/7 East 48 Street, New York, N.Y. 10017

Contents

To the memory of my Father

'I strove with none; for none was worth my strife;
Nature I loved, and, next to Nature, Art;
I warm'd both hands before the fire of life;
It sinks, and I am ready to depart.'
—WALTER SAVAGE LANDOR

Introduction

It's been said that all authors are frustrated adventurers at heart. Since I boast a few books to my name I subscribe to that view—particularly about one book—this book. But I'll start at the beginning.

One midnight a rumbling muse got cracking. My progeny? The great idea. I would write a book on Marlene Dietrich, the wistful languorous Marlene, that literate and most untouchable of women, the legend and the lie. I grew enthusiastic. The more I burrowed, the more gleeful I grew to discover that no one—but no one—had ever written a book about Marlene. But that's a lie, for a start. Somebody had. A Teutonic journalist in her native Germany had written a slim volume shortly after *The Blue Angel*. But few people knew about it.

I went to work. A summer sped swiftly like a life to its close. I worked. I smoked. I researched. And smoked some more. I went to Berlin, Austria, Paris and Regent's Park. My publisher sat on my neck. For published my book was—but not without such agony of authorship as I had never before known.

Strange things happen when you write a book about a living person. I hadn't got to Chapter Five before I was the recipient of a series of curious telephone calls. A man who claimed he was a Major Someone rang me and advised me that I was 'on dangerous ground'. And had I asked Miss Dietrich's permission? I told him no, but that I proposed to send her the manuscript for her comments. Why did I want to write a book about her? he asked. Many people had tried but had never got into print. I said I wanted to know what made the lady tick. And I proposed to find

out. 'Ah,' he said sinisterly, 'but I strongly advise you not to do
it. Take my advice, dear boy . . .'

Two posts later my publishers received a letter from Miss Dietrich from a Park Avenue address—one could almost smell the perfume. Miss Dietrich said she'd heard and that we mustn't. My
publisher said, 'but we must', and we'd show her the ms and she
could make suggestions and then everybody would be happy.
Somebody else telephoned to say that the only person she would
allow to write the book would be Noël Coward. And he hadn't
been asked.

All of which seemed to coincide with Miss Dietrich's arrival in
London a week later for her fabulous season at the old Café de
Paris. My telephone rang again. It was Kenneth Tynan. Was it true,
he asked, that I was writing a book about the lady? Guilty, said I.
'Well, I think you ought to reconsider . . .' Here we went again,
this from a writer who can write and whom one would have imagined believed in that elusive thing called 'artistic freedom'. But
no matter.

Mischa Spoliansky, the composer, for long a much respected
chum, intervened. I had interviewed him about Miss Dietrich,
the worthy ex-Fräulein, his friend of many years. He obviously
didn't want me to say what he had said. Then one evening I got
a message to ring a Hampstead number. No name, no packdrill.
I was about to ask for whomever had been asking for me when I
heard those unmistakable sultry feminine chords—she might just
as well have sung a few bars from *Falling in Love Again.* 'Who is
that?' said the voice. 'Forgive me,' I replied, 'but who is *that*—I'm
trying to establish who telephoned *me . . .*'

'Please tell me your name. Your name *please*,' she said urgently
—as if she didn't know. Well, I thought, if this is the lark, let's
both play. And play we did. And we talked for five minutes until
finally—because she had obviously asked a friend to get me to
phone the Hampstead telephone number as Miss Dietrich didn't

want to phone me *directly*—we both got nowhere fast. In desperation, she said in guttural tones 'Please have the courtesy to tell me your name. For the last time, who are you?' I said: 'It doesn't really matter, Miss Dietrich,' and hung up.

By now the pressure was really on. It happened that I was writing for a major movie company. I was summoned to the edifice. The boss man wanted me. He took five minutes to get around to it. Then he said: 'Er, this book of yours—how much do you expect to make out of it?' I replied that he'd better ask my agent. 'Roughly,' he insisted. 'Oh, about five thousand,' I said, snatching a figure out of space. That really shook him.

He finally offered me £350 to abandon the book. And he never told me *why* he'd made the offer. The overall campaign tactics were, I deemed, a little clumsy. I thought that perhaps one ought to look into this business of artistic freedom. After all, my lawyer had told the lady that we none of us had any wish to offend, that my admiration for her was profound, and that she could see the ms . . . Then the late Nancy Spain stepped in. And, poor lass, she didn't stop. She flung words, veiled threats and oaths around like a threshing machine.

I dug my heels in. Then my erstwhile and long-time friend Charles Graves, a writer of considerable talent and acumen, telephoned me. I might have been talking to Tynan because they both said the same thing. And, in reply, so did I. No, I would *not* abandon the book. Sorry, chum.

And then the movie boss who was bigger than the other big boss, summoned me to his chamber of horrors. I remember that he had the longest couch I ever saw, right along one wall of his office. The dialogue was much the same. An opening about my health and future. And then—the book. Didn't I think I ought to abandon it? No, I said, I didn't. He made it fairly obvious that I was from that moment on out of favour. The pressurisers were now in full sail. The Big Chief, bigger than the first one, even enlisted his smooth PRO who interviewed the star—and came back and got to work on me on the side, and didn't have a clue that I already knew that he'd found the lady . . . 'My dear old fruit,' he said—yes, he actually did say that—'I reckon this book business is a dead loss. We've got lots of plans for you . . .' I told him in, I hope, impeccable English where his future lay if he continued to interfere, and went home to telephone my publisher.

Well, let's just say that he, too, had changed. I thought I'd written a pretty reasonable book, honest, if not brilliant, truthful, if not sagacious. But it seemed the lawyers had said—take this out, take that out—and it had all been taken out so that when I got the galley proofs I knew the day was over and that night was drawing nigh.

Eminent people, famous people, infamous people, took such an insatiable interest in my writing activities during that sad summer, people whom I never even knew had heard of me.

Mark you, no one ever really said anything *definite*—but I planned to stick to war stories after it all. At least, I reasoned, I could write about big guns with a certain degree of intimate knowledge.

That was in 1955—some aeons ago, it seems. But, like a faithful spaniel, I still love the lady. And I remain with a high regard and interest in this most permanent of glamorous grandmothers. Thus, I decided a short time ago, I would bring *Blond Venus* up to date. I would research and re-write to see how she stood up in The Swinging Sixties. And I'd publish it myself.

I think she's way ahead of the Jet Set, the nubile nonentities and the synthetic sycophants of the Silver Screen of 1967. And, despite the roar of the greasepaint she is, to me, still the loveliest woman I've ever seen. And a mistress of her art.

I hope this book will prove just that—and more, perhaps.

CHAPTER ONE

Infancy

'A charming union.' This had been the verdict of Berlin society on the marriage of Major Louis Dietrich, of the lance-bearing cavalry, and Fräulein Felsing, whose father was head of the famous Conrad Felsing jewellery concern, founded by his grandfather. The 'charming union', which always observed strict aristocratic principles of sober conduct and propriety, produced two children, both girls: Elizabeth, with brownish hair and startling eyes, and flaxen-haired Maria Magdalene, who arrived a little earlier than the doctor expected on the morning of the 27th December 1904.

Shortly before the birth of his second daughter, Major Dietrich had been ordered to Weimar; it was in the capital of the Grand Duchy of Saxe-Weimar-Eisenach, near the river Ilm, that the life of Maria Magdalene began—Maria Magdalene who, years later, was to elide the syllables of her Christian names to become Marlene Dietrich, star of extraordinary and lasting brilliance in films, and a legend in her own time.

Frau Dietrich's favourite relaxation was music. She was a good classical pianist, she sang madrigals and traditional German songs. She believed that Maria Magdalene had musical talent, and arranged for her to start piano and violin lessons at an early age.

The Dietrich family loved Berlin, and on Major Dietrich's death when his daughters were still in their childhood, they continued to live there. Maria, accompanied by a stout Alsatian servant, would cross the Kurfürstendamm each morning to practise her scales at the house of a distinguished old lady, Frau Dessant.

With her bachelor brother, Frau Dessant taught the sons and daughters of Berlin society artistic appreciation, and gave Maria a regular piano and violin lesson. In the afternoon, after lunch with her parents, Maria would be given a short walk and then handed over to her English governess. Sometimes, if the weather was fine, she would accompany her mother on visits. The child was never told in advance on whom her mother proposed to call, and knew that it was none of her business to ask, for the Prussian discipline of the household was never perceptibly relaxed. It was an essential principle of that society and, naturally, it erected artificial barriers between parents and children.

Maria was a pretty child, her hair delicately dressed in ribbons. 'Isn't she a charming child?' was a remark she often heard at the house of a family friend, and, as she had been taught, received impassively. Impassively, too, she accepted kisses from old ladies, acknowledging them with a formal outstretched hand and always the same remark, repeated in a grave little voice: 'Good day, Madame. I hope you are well?'

Occasionally discipline broke down. Presented one day with a doll by one of her mother's friends, she was instructed to repay the kindness with a kiss. Disliking the old lady, whom she found peculiarly unattractive, Maria declined. The command was repeated, Maria still did not move; the situation could only be resolved by Frau Dietrich taking her from the room and walking her sternly home. The incident was duly considered; the child was punished; and Maria did not refuse a kiss again.

She learned also how to go without an overcoat when the winter was bitterly cold and how to refrain from asking for a glass of water when she was almost aching from thirst. She listened to family lectures on the virtue of never wasting food, of always maintaining self-possession and concealing any mood of unhappiness or discontent. All this, it was explained, was to strengthen her character against slackness or apathy. No doubt her riding lessons, another regular part of her education, came as a release. She was often in the Tiergarten, an army private with a leading rein mounted beside her; she laughed with secret glee at young officers who ogled as she passed, and told Elizabeth about it afterwards.

By the time she was ten, family discipline was not the only pressure. International tension was rising, the Imperial Prussian Army was being mobilised, and the royal sentries were no longer wearing their elaborate peace-time uniforms. After the outbreak of war, Frau Dietrich married again. Her second husband was also a soldier, Lieutenant Edouard von Losch of the König Regiment, which was considered the kernel of the Prussian Army by German nobility, and accepted only men from the best families. Tall, with finely modelled features and typical Prussian bearing, Lieutenant von Losch fitted the military regime to perfection; when he married Frau Dietrich, he came to live in the large, old-fashioned house that Louis had left her, and its rigorous traditions were maintained. But the war meant that Marlene scarcely came to know her stepfather. This family separation apart, the war at first made little impact on the quiet residential section of Berlin in which the Dietrich (now von Losch) family lived, and there was no relaxation in the routine of the girls' lives. Maria's eight-hour day included French and English lessons now, and she was becoming perfect in both languages. She showed, as yet, no interest in acting. Years later, discussing her early life, she remarked: 'My mother made acting difficult for me. My whole upbringing was to mask my feelings—the last slap I had from my mother was because of that. I was having dancing lessons, and had to dance with everyone in the room, including a young man I did not like. I made a long face. Mother saw it and slapped me as soon as we were alone. "You must not show your feelings, it is bad manners," she said.'

In 1916, writing home from the French front, Edouard von Losch felt certain of a resounding German victory and expected to be entering Paris in a few weeks. A week later he was transferred to command a sector along the Russian border. Like so many, he did not realise the seriousness of a threat on two fronts, nor the full effectiveness of the Allied blockade. It was this blockade which first made Frau von Losch and other Berliners begin to doubt the invincibility of the German war machine. Luxuries became non-existent, then necessities; there was no meat—potatoes and turnips became the main diet. Steadily, news of the deaths of relatives reached her. Then, early in 1918, word came that Edouard, now promoted Colonel, had been seriously wounded in a skirmish on the Russian front near Kowel, a bullet shattering his shoulder and arm.

At the evacuation hospital she found him still alive and full of quiet concern for herself and the children. The doctors were guardedly hopeful; but as she waited, he had a sudden relapse. For several days he grew weaker. Once, on his sickbed, he turned to his wife and whispered: 'Maria must be a great musician.' She nodded comfortingly. 'I will see to it, Edouard.'

He clung to life for a few more days with grim and characteristic tenacity. After the funeral Frau von Losch returned to Berlin and her daughters, a widow again.

CHAPTER TWO

Youth

Maria and Elizabeth were saddened by the death of their step-father, severe disciplinarian though he had been. Without him, the family seemed small and lost, and the last year of the war, in the large old-fashioned house, was a melancholy one. When peace came, it seemed that everything in the old order had changed: hunger, unrest, rioting in the streets, and a hard, cold winter—these things put an end to the solid charm and contentment of upper-middle-class life in Berlin.

With the drop in the mark, too, Frau von Losch's personal fortune had dwindled alarmingly. She decided to sell the house, and moved with her daughters to a small, unpretentious flat. Maria was sent off almost immediately to Weimar, her birthplace, to finish her education at a boarding-school and continue her music studies. The child's tutors considered that she displayed talent, and it was now taken for granted that Maria would become a concert violinist.

The Berlin that Maria left was not the city of her childhood. The innumerable poor and unemployed crowded into the cheap dance halls and cafés that were springing up everywhere; and even their pleasures—the tinny, incessant ragtime bands to which soldiers and their girlfriends danced, the cabaret songs with their cynical, weary lyrics—seemed to reflect a profound and ominous social disturbance.

Weimar, by contrast, still maintained its quiet respectability, was still famous, among other things, for its superior girls' schools.

Maria was happy there; for two years she studied under Professor Flesch, her music teacher, who firmly believed she would become a great violinist; and she read a great deal of poetry, particularly Hofmannsthal, Goethe and Rilke. From time to time she received letters from her mother, but they were not very communicative. It was not until Maria returned to Berlin in 1921, to enter the *Hochschule für Musik*, the State musical academy, to take her final examinations, that she discovered the extent of unrest in the city and the small income to which her mother had been reduced.

All household expenditure in the little flat now had to be carefully watched. As a result of hardship, perhaps, Frau von Losch had become less aloof, and the family reunion resulted in a closer, more intimate affection between mother and daughter. Maria worked hard at the Academy, and made good progress. Then, one day, she complained of a constant pain in her left hand, near the wrist. A doctor was consulted.

'What does she do?' he asked Frau von Losch.

'She is studying the violin at the *Hochschule*.'

'She must give it up,' the doctor said. 'Immediately.'

Neither mother nor daughter realised, at first, that the doctor meant she must give up the violin for good. But he was insistent. Maria's constant practice had developed a ganglion—an enlargement or knot—on the primary nerve of her left wrist.

For a few days Maria had no idea what to do. The main purpose of her life had suddenly vanished. She was still under twenty, untrained for any profession, and it was certainly impossible for her to continue living at home without helping to provide for the family. When she took stock of herself, her endowments for facing life in post-war Berlin did not seem impressive. A talent for music which she could not exercise: a good traditional upbringing: a taste for the arts: proficiency in French and English . . . And there were few people to whom she could turn for advice.

The decision she finally made was instinctive, not reasoned. Near the Schumannstrasse was Max Reinhardt's Deutsches Theatre, the centre of theatre art in Berlin and the home of the *avant-garde*. Next door to it was Reinhardt's theatre school, known as *Friedrichs Gymnasium*. It was this little world that Maria decided to conquer.

CHAPTER THREE

A Visit to Reinhardt

When Maria, after several attempts, finally obtained an interview
with Reinhardt, she told him quite simply that she wanted to go
on the stage. As quickly as possible, she added. Sitting at his desk,
Reinhardt stared across at the pretty, plumpish girl. He seemed
friendly, perhaps intrigued by her directness, and asked without
surprise what experience she had had. 'None,' Maria told him. The
producer, no doubt, was ready for this too. He told her to leave
her address, and he would see what could be done.

Maria went home elated. The great man had seen her, talked
to her, and given her, it seemed, at least a degree of hope. At tea
she broke the news to her mother.

'I want,' she said, using almost the same words that she had
spoken to Reinhardt, 'to go on the stage.'

Frau von Losch's reaction was characteristic. Maria, she pointed
out, was a young girl from good society. The stage was infamous.
The idea must be renounced.

No more, for the moment, was said. But Maria returned to the
Deutsches Theatre building a few days later, and encountered
Reinhardt, with two colleagues, on the stairs. She asked him when
he was going to let her start. This time he hardly glanced at her,
only said, 'You are not ready,' and passed on without hearing her
eager denial.

'I hear you were seen near the Deutsches Theatre today, Maria.
Why were you there? Did you go to see Reinhardt?'

It would be no use denying it, Maria told herself. She explained to her mother that family disgrace would be averted because she had given herself a new name. 'It is a little of Maria and a little of Magdalene. And it is my father's name too. I have called myself Marlene Dietrich.'

She had been Marlene Dietrich, in fact, since her first interview with Reinhardt, for it was the name she had written down for him. Frau von Losch, however, showed no signs of relenting; and it became necessary for her daughter to practise a deception. Marlene, as the theatre now knew her, began secretly to attend auditions, and it was not long before she was offered a job in a Hamburg chorus. She told her mother she was going to Hamburg to visit some friends.

She enjoyed the visit. The audiences appreciated her, and Marlene received a number of compliments on her beautiful legs. She put so much energy into her work that the girl next to her in the chorus line was constantly telling her not to sing so loudly. And she was suddenly reminded of something the family cook had said to her in the old days: 'If I had a voice like yours, Fräulein, I wouldn't go on shouting for the rest of my life. You have nice legs—but legs don't talk. You should take a lesson from your legs . . .'

When the show finished, Marlene returned to Berlin, and was overjoyed by an offer from Reinhardt to join his company. He had a very small part for her in his forthcoming production of *The Taming of the Shrew*. There was, as it turned out, no opportunity to shine, and not one of the critics mentioned her; but it felt like an exciting start, and she was now enrolled as a student at Reinhardt's school. Marlene was beginning to develop a passion for the theatre. Although films were becoming increasingly popular, she took little interest in them; although she went to the cinema quite often, admired Emil Jannings, Conrad Veidt and Dolly Haas, she believed it to be a second-rate medium for the real actor. Her ideal was Elisabeth Bergner. That was what she wanted to become—a great and famous stage actress like *Lisel* Bergner.

There were, however, practical considerations. Becoming an actress had involved 'leaving home', and Marlene now had to support herself. Most of Reinhardt's young pupils earned a little money on the side by appearing as extras in films, and one of them pointed out to Marlene that nearly all the great actors at the Deutsches and elsewhere, even Bergner, also worked in the cinema.

Consoled, she followed suit. One day, between going the rounds of agents' and managers' offices, she formed her first real friendship.

A girl called Gerda Huber, with ambitions to become a journalist, had gone to lunch at a small, cheap, crowded restaurant. While she waited for her meal, she heard a voice ask: 'May I sit here with you?' The young woman who sat down opposite had dark gold hair screwed up into a bun at the nape of her neck, and, Gerda considered, no idea how to dress. She ordered a pork chop with vegetables, and proceeded to eat it ravenously.

Gerda watched her. 'Aren't you afraid,' she said at last, 'of getting fat if you eat as much as that?'

Marlene Dietrich looked a little surprised. 'Do you think I'm fat? When it's cold and I'm worried, I get terribly hungry. This may be my last good meal for weeks.'

It seemed now to Gerda, who was out of a job and whose savings were practically finished, that she had met a kindred spirit.

'My savings are *completely* finished,' Marlene informed her. 'I've left home, and I'm not even sure where I'm going to sleep tonight.'

When Gerda asked about her circumstances and her family, Marlene was evasive. She was an actress, she said, making her way on her own, and she would not speak about her parents. She struck Gerda as practical but rather romantic about herself.

'I must find a job in Berlin,' Marlene said, now eating an apple. 'I've had a fairly good education, I've read a good deal, so I ought to be able to get something worth while.'

By the end of the meal the two girls had become friends. Gerda suggested that Marlene should come and live at her *pension*, where the kind-hearted landlady would certainly give her credit for a month.

'The best thing that could happen to me, you know,' Marlene said very earnestly, as they approached the front door, 'would be to find a good husband.' Gerda laughed, but Marlene insisted: 'And I shouldn't mind if he owned a farm, and then we could live in the country and keep ducks and chickens and pigs, and have nothing to worry about . . .'

Marlene lived at the *pension* for several months. She quickly endeared herself to Trude, the amiable landlady, by her passion for Puck, the *pension* cat, a fat, striped creature with long and gentle whiskers. 'I'm sure,' she said, 'cats bring me good luck.' Although Puck gave her no reason to believe this, she was devoted to him, and sat with him for long hours while she read a book or mended Gerda's stockings.

These were difficult times. The girls had little money, few prospects, and Marlene used to worry about the shabbiness of Gerda's wardrobe. However, if Gerda lacked clothes, she did not lack taste; and this was a subject on which they frequently disagreed. Marlene would often see something in a shop window of which Gerda disapproved. Gerda insisted that Marlene should dress plainly, even severely, to suit her figure, and while Marlene agreed in principle, she could seldom resist sticking a superfluous feather in her hat or tying an outsize bow to a frock.

Marlene seemed, at this time, oddly changeable and capricious in her moods. She earned little money—occasional work as a film extra and once, when times were particularly bad, a few weeks at a glove factory. A letter from her mother would make her preoccupied with her failure to send any money home. She spent a great deal of time indoors, reading, with Puck at her side, and sometimes helping Trude to cook. She went to the theatre with Gerda, as often as they could afford to, watching every performance intently and discussing it eagerly afterwards. They went less frequently to the cinema, which she still did not care for, finding the popular German 'vamps' particularly absurd.

One day Gerda arranged to meet her in the park. As she waited near the bandstand, Marlene ran up, breathless and excited. She gave a radiant smile, and told Gerda she had been playing with some ragged children. Gerda remonstrated with her, but Marlene only laughed, took her arm, waved to the children, and bought some roast chestnuts at a stall. As she walked along, she threw the skins to the wind.

But a few evenings later she was sitting in her room, hunched over an oil stove, reading a letter. Puck was on her knees. When Gerda came in, she said: 'I feel I'll never be a success. I shan't find a husband, I shan't be able to earn a living. I'm no good at anything.'

Gerda tried to console her, then suggested that Trude should tell her fortune with the cards. This was one of the landlady's favourite pastimes, which the girls took lightly enough, but tonight Marlene seemed engrossed by it. As Trude prophesied an adventurous future, with travel and riches and a promising encounter with an Eastern potentate, she became nervous and irritated. 'But don't you see whether I'm going to get married or not?' she asked.

Trude consulted the cards, and announced that her marriage would not be important.

'Shall I have any children?'

'Perhaps. But it's not the thing that matters. You will be a rich woman.'

Marlene seemed to become almost angry at this, and the card reading ended.

At about this time, too, something else momentarily disillusioned her. 'Marlene was never lacking admirers,' Gerda has since recalled, 'but they were generally rather vulgar—people who liked the look of her when they saw her in the street or on a tram.' Marlene accepted such admiration lightly, but there was one man more persistent than the others. 'To do him justice,' Gerda has said, 'he saw in her what no one else at that time had seen—that she could develop into a real beauty. He was a rich, elderly man with a swollen neck, who'd made a lot of money during the war.'

Although Gerda disliked him, she felt that he might help Marlene, and urged her to see him. One evening she overheard a fragment of conversation in his car.

'I'll turn you into the prettiest little girl in Berlin,' he was telling her. 'I'll furnish a wonderful flat for you. You can have jewels, furs, everything you want . . .'

But when she came home that night, Marlene seemed dejected. 'When I'm really desperate, this old man will be my last resort,' she said. Then she smiled rather bitterly. 'You see, Gerda, I'm after a *permanent* situation.'

Not long afterwards she learned that the man had a wife and two young children. She flew into a rage, and cried bitterly.

CHAPTER FOUR

Meeting Rudolph Sieber

It was the energetic Gerda who was the first to find something relatively 'permanent'. She was given a job on the editorial staff of a newspaper in Hanover. This meant, of course, leaving Marlene, and she was uneasy about it. Would she, with her gentle and sensitive nature, survive the harsh realities of Berlin in the twenties? What would happen to the girl with the unsuitable red hat and the tears forming in her eyes as the train steamed out of the station?

For a while, to judge from Marlene's letters, life went on as before. Then, for many months, Marlene stopped writing—and when, at last, another letter came, Gerda was alarmed.

'Gerda, do you remember me? I'm still continuing my theatrical career, but without hope of getting much further in it, without hope of ever becoming a good actress. I might as well try to reach the moon. I suppose the life itself is neither better nor worse than lots of others, but it's so different from the one I ought to have chosen for myself . . . You can imagine the kind of people and the surroundings with which I am involved. I feel so miserable, so sick of everything. I have a part in a play at the moment, a better one, though it is very small. I'm not living with Trude any more—I've found a *pension* that is more central, nearer the theatre. Puck is with me, and we're going to live like this for ever and ever . . .'

Disappointment, it seemed, had cruelly sapped her once lively ambitions. The only work Marlene could get at this time was a series of brief stage parts, little better than 'walk-ons'—even though one of them was in a play starring her idol, Elisabeth Bergner—and an occasional day's employment in the film studios.

The German cinema in 1923 was beginning to capture world attention. The success of *The Cabinet of Dr Caligari* and of Ernst Lubitsch's lavish historical films had encouraged a succession of macabre fantasies and period melodramas, rhetorically acted and theatrically designed in a manner inspired by Reinhardt's successes on the stage. At the UFA studios twenty miles outside Berlin, there was a formidable concentration of talent—among actors, Jannings, Veidt, Fritz Kortner, Werner Krauss, Oscar Homolka, Franz Lederer, Lil Dagover, and among directors, Fritz Lang, Murnau and Pabst.

One day Marlene was called to the UFA studios as an extra in a big costume film. On these occasions she was always diffident, as she had discovered that she photographed badly—her golden hair looked lifeless and her grey-blue eyes appeared too pale, almost white. The assistant director, however, was a polite and good-looking young Sudeten-Czech called Rudolph Sieber. He thrust a lorgnette into her hand and told her: 'You are to act like a young duchess.'

Marlene recalls the incident: 'I had some experience of elderly duchesses, but not of younger ones. Still, I caricatured the type as well as I could. But it was the lorgnette that attracted the director most—he focused the camera on it, which meant, of course, that he *had* to photograph my face.'

The lorgnette made what is known as a 'halation'—a spot of light reflected into the camera lens and magnified by the image. Today, cameramen always avoid halations, but it was the kind of light effect appropriate to the style of the German silent cinema, and the director liked it. The shot remained in the film. Sieber, also, found Marlene interesting. He thought she had charm and dramatic possibilities, and mentioned her to Joe May, a successful

27

director of the time, who gave her a small part in his next film, *Die Tragodie der Liebe*, which starred Jannings as a Parisian prize-fighter in love with a chambermaid. The film was a success, but once again nothing came of it for Marlene.

Meanwhile, Gerda returned to Berlin. She had heard nothing from Marlene since the last despairing letter, and was unable to find her new address. One evening she went to see a Gloria Swanson film—and when the lights went up found she had been sitting next to her friend.

'Gloria Swanson,' Marlene said. 'Now, there's someone who isn't beautiful but a thousand times better than beautiful.'

Marlene, it seemed to Gerda, had matured. Her high cheek-bones were more noticeable; her figure looked slimmer, more feminine and pronounced. But she didn't give the impression of being happy, and when Gerda began asking questions, she became despondent. She still, theoretically, wanted to get married, but there was no man she cared for. 'Are you never going to fall in love?' Gerda asked. Marlene smiled. 'Yes,' she said, 'but Puck has gone off with a lady cat, and he hasn't come back!'

Two old habits, however, were unchanged: a hearty appetite, and a taste for atrocious hats.

Shortly after Gerda returned, Marlene was signed to appear in a revue. She had to sing, dance and wear a scanty costume. The audience liked her, and once more her legs were singled out for special praise. But when Gerda went round to her dressing-room one night after the show, she found her friend depressed. It was 'agony', Marlene said. When the audience stared at her, it was a kind of torture; she couldn't stand it, she wanted to run away.

On the last night, the manager of a popular music hall came round with the offer of a contract. Marlene, walking up and down with a sequin-covered cloak wrapped round her body, seemed uneasy while he talked. She protested that she wasn't a singer or a dancer, but an actress. The manager advised her to be realistic. 'As an actress you might easily go on only playing small parts, but in the music hall you would be seen to advantage . . .'

In spite of reports to the contrary, Marlene did not sign this contract, and she was not to appear in music halls or night clubs until many years later. When the manager had gone, she took her friend's arm. 'Let's eat,' she said, 'shall we?'

CHAPTER FIVE

Marriage

One evening, when Gerda was helping Marlene cook supper at her *pension,* the maid brought in a visiting card. It bore the name of Rudolph Sieber.

Marlene seemed pleased. She introduced him to Gerda and described the incident with the lorgnette at the UFA studios. Sieber said that his company was preparing a new film, and had a small part which would be good for her. He didn't stay long, but during those few minutes Gerda's intuition told her that Marlene was interested in the eager, friendly young man. For the moment, however, she said nothing.

A few days later her job took her away from Berlin for nearly four months, and when she returned to the *pension* she found Marlene in the middle of cooking a meal. The table was set for two. 'Rudolph is coming tonight,' Marlene said. 'The first time he has ever been to dinner with me.'

She seemed happier, more light-hearted than she had been for a long time. Her career was still marking time, she had just been given another small part in a film, and she was sure she was going to photograph badly again. But this time she laughed about it. 'I'm too fat, and my face looks like a potato!'

It was clear that Rudolph Sieber was more important to her now. And the next day Marlene went round to Gerda's lodgings to tell her friend that she had just agreed to become his wife. She was radiant. When Gerda asked her if she would still continue her acting career, she only shrugged and smiled. 'It will have to take care of itself. All I know is, Rudolph is the only man who has understood me and cared for me in the right way . . .'

Marlene's sudden, almost triumphant indifference to her film career was something that few of her friends could understand. She had met many people at the studios by this time, and there seemed a good chance that if she persevered the cinema might soon begin to take real notice of her. But at this moment all she cared about was personal happiness.

She married Rudolph Sieber in 1925. They set up home together, they were seen everywhere together, dining and dancing. One evening he took her to a night club which was popular with theatre and film people. At a nearby table was a dark, spectacled Hungarian, Alexander Korda, whose lavish film of *Samson and Delilah* had just earned a great success. A production manager at UFA's Babelsberg studios walked in with a companion. The production manager was Victor Skutezsky, and his companion was E A Dupont, whose *Variety* was then playing in the cinemas. Skutezsky noticed the beautiful blonde girl with a fair-haired young man.

'I noticed the girl,' he said later, 'but I noticed her legs first. I turned to Dupont—but he had already greeted her. I asked him who she was, and he told me her name was Marlene Dietrich and she'd already had a bit part in one of our films.'

Skutezsky remembered the name—and the legs. Two years later he was working on a film for UFA, *Manner vor der Ehe*, and looking for a girl to play a small part, about which there was a special directive from the producer. The role demanded someone with 'long and beautiful legs'. Skutezsky contacted Marlene, who came to his office, listened to his explanation of the part, and calmly demanded two hundred marks (then equivalent to £10) a day for the five days' work involved. Skutezsky told her that the budget wouldn't permit him to pay that much for a minor actress who was required to do little more than show off her legs. Marlene turned the offer down.

More than twenty years later Victor Skutezsky was to establish himself as a producer in Britain. Shortly after World War Two he offered Marlene Dietrich another role—a starring one this time, of course, in the film of Georges Simenon's *Temptation Harbour*. 'I offered her *infinitely* more than £10 a day,' he recalls, 'for the part eventually played by Simone Simon. But she turned it down just the same. I am certainly one of the few people who can truthfully claim *not* to have discovered Marlene Dietrich.'

But soon after she rejected Skutezsky's first offer, a very important event occurred in Marlene Dietrich's life. She gave birth to her first and only child—a daughter.

CHAPTER SIX

Family and the Theatre

Marlene has described the months following the birth of her daughter Maria as 'the happiest of my life.' She idolised the child, and was a devoted, conscientious mother. Far more important than acting now was converting the biggest room in the flat into a nursery. With conditions in Berlin changing for the better—the mark rising again, food prices becoming stabilised—the family of three was able to live comfortably enough on Rudolph's salary.

But it was not long before friends were urging her to resume her stage career. She had achieved some success in one of her small film parts (*The Great Baritone*, starring Albert Basserman), and producers were enquiring about her. The theatre in Berlin was now busy and prosperous, and when Marlene decided to heed her friends' advice, she was almost immediately offered a sizable part in a musical play called *Broadway*.

When the producer called her for an interview, he asked Marlene if she could dance. With the new confidence that a happy marriage and motherhood had given her, Marlene would now have cheerfully answered that she could speak Chinese or perform conjuring tricks. She was told to report for rehearsal the next day.

Broadway was an American musical that has since been performed all over the world. It had a New York night club setting and a gangster story; Marlene played the girlfriend of a gangster who is killed and whose death she avenges. The part gave her some dramatic scenes, two numbers to sing, and some dances in which she displayed her shapely legs. It was a moderate success, and she followed it with a good part in a new Reinhardt production, *Es Leigt in der Luft*. Robert Land, a film producer, saw her in this and approached her with the offer of a small part in a new film. Marlene was still uninterested in this kind of work, and regarded films as something to help out the household budget when necessary. At the moment she was not short of money, and she wanted to continue in the theatre. But Land persisted, and she finally agreed to play the role in *Prinzess in Olala* (later shown in Britain under the title *The Art of Love*), based on a popular operetta by Franz Schultz.

It is worth noting here that in all these early films Marlene was invited to play either women of the world or girls clearly untroubled by conventional sexual morality. She was in fact to continue with this kind of characterisation for most of her screen career. In *Prinzess in Olala*, which starred Walter Rilla, the part was not very long but it provided the chief feminine interest. Land was pleased with her work, and even before the film came out decided he had a 'discovery' on his hands. He offered her a leading role in his next production, *Ich Kusse Ihre Hand, Madame*, which she accepted.

Both these films gained her some warm critical notices. As a film actress, Marlene Dietrich was beginning to taste success. New offers arrived in increasing numbers, and in 1929 she made her third important film, which was later to enjoy a six weeks' run at the New York Playhouse under the title *Three Loves*. She starred with Fritz Kortner and Uno Henning, and the director was Kurt Bernhardt, later to change his Christian name to Curtis and make a successful career in Hollywood.

After this, Marlene could do what she really wanted: return to the stage. She played the lead in Shaw's *Misalliance*, and it was the kind of opportunity for which she had waited so long. For the first time in her career she felt that the signals were set in her favour. And she had met her idol, Elisabeth Bergner.

Enthusiastic critics, indeed, were even beginning to mention both actresses in the same breath, and many of them advised her to give up the screen and concentrate on the theatre. Before she could do this, however, she had a film contract to fulfil, and she appeared in *Das Schiff der Verlorenen Menschen* (*The Ship of Lost Men*), with Kortner again, and Gaston Modot. The director this time was Maurice Tourneur, who had already made films with Mary Pickford in Hollywood, and was shortly to work in France with Raimu and Harry Baur.

The tide had turned, and Marlene Dietrich was becoming a successful, well-known actress. She was also a happy woman now, in love with her husband and devoted to her young daughter. She had money and friends, and she enjoyed social life. In 1929, she no longer looked anxiously to the future; the present was good enough.

She was soon to learn, however, that the future was looking to her.

CHAPTER SEVEN

Something in the Air

While there was no doubt of her talent, there were critics and producers in Berlin who had reservations about Marlene Dietrich's ability as an actress of the Bergner class. One of the most imaginative producers in Germany at that time was Victor Barnowsky, whose work in the Viennese theatre had gained him a reputation second only to Reinhardt's. Some years later he recollected the Dietrich of this period:

'Marlene Dietrich was a fine actress in the making. She was superlatively beautiful—too beautiful, it seemed to me. "*Beautiful I was, too, and that my undoing,*" says Gretchen in *Faust*. Many people in the theatre in Berlin believed that extreme beauty and first-class acting talent never went together, and it seemed at that time as if Marlene's loveliness might prove an eventual disadvantage.

'When I first met her, Marlene was very young, dazzlingly fresh, elegant, supremely good-looking, and with a touch of "feyness" that made her slightly mysterious. But she lacked self-confidence, and seemed unaware of her many attractions—except, perhaps, of her legs. The admiration they frequently excited in restaurants and public places would startle her at least into a certain self-consciousness. Also, she was very much the well-brought-up young lady, passionately fond of music—a passion as essential to her personality as her desire to play tragic roles.

'I can see her now, in a copper-coloured silk dress, leaning against the wall of my office during an audition, reciting lines from some sentimental play, the name of which I've forgotten. It was an arresting sight—but could she have been aware of the effect she was creating?

'In a comparatively short time, however, she was transformed. I couldn't tell whether she was reacting dynamically to a new and strange environment, or whether she was experiencing some fundamental development within herself. Whatever it was, she became the prototype of the *diable de femme*. I remember meeting her at a gay pre-Lenten costume ball. More beautiful than ever, strikingly like a portrait by Toulouse-Lautrec, she moved graciously among the dancers . . .

'Her first audition for me was successful, and when she began rehearsals for *Back to Methuselah* she threw herself heart and soul into the part. Even so, she seemed sadly lacking in that inner fire which should have been the complement of her physical charms. She was in sharp contrast to Elisabeth Bergner, who as a beginner displayed apparent physical helplessness, and yet seemed to hold something ultimate, something mysterious in reserve.

'One day I was discussing Dietrich with Bergner and extolling her beauty. Bergner agreed warmly, but after a moment asked me —with a slight twinkle in her eye and a mock anxiety in her voice —if I didn't think that she too was "just a little bit too beautiful". I replied with a line from *Romeo and Juliet*:

> *Alack, there lies more peril in thine eye*
> *Than twenty of their swords* . . .

'And Bergner said: "If I were as beautiful as Dietrich, I shouldn't know what to do with my talent." '

In 1936, when Dietrich had become an international star, Barnowsky was to add to his comments:

'In Marlene Dietrich the theatre has lost a jewel which has found its natural setting in the cinema. A child of her time, Mar-

37

lene has become the reflection, the model, the symbol, of the alluring woman—the vamp, the *femme fatale* or whatever you like to
call it. Garbo is the symbol of enduring womanhood, inspiring
alike in divine or devilish mood, and Bergner is the ideal of the
modern girl, mysterious and indefinable. Perhaps Marlene will be
the type of tomorrow . . .'

In 1929 Marlene made another film, *Liebesnächte*, in which she
played opposite Willy Först. Once again her figure and her legs
were knowingly exploited; but it was difficult to know what she
really felt about this, whether perhaps she still experienced an element of that alarm which had sometimes overwhelmed her on
previous occasions. Walter Rilla remembers filming at UFA when
Dietrich was on the set. Two or three actors were standing beside
her while they waited for the completion of a shot. Besides Marlene, the film in the making included three young girls of considerable physical appeal. The conversation turned to their
charms, and Marlene suddenly turned round and raised her skirts
above her knees.

'I have good legs too,' she said. 'Haven't I? . . .'

While Marlene was making this film, Reinhardt was preparing a
stage production of Somerset Maugham's *Home and Beauty*. He
had made considerable alterations to the script, and approached a
young composer, Mischa Spoliansky, to set the production to
music. This musical version was called *Viktoria*, and Spoliansky's
score earned him considerable acclaim.

Reinhardt followed it with another musical production, a revue
to be called *Something in the Air*, for which Spoliansky again
wrote the music and Marlene Dietrich was auditioned for a part.

Marlene had originally met Spoliansky shortly after her marriage to Rudolph Sieber. His tunes were at that time beginning to
have a success in cabaret, and one night he played a new foxtrot

for the first time at the Boston Club, when Marlene and her husband were there. Later, Marlene introduced herself and told him how much she liked it.

Spoliansky thanked her, and asked: 'What did you say your name was?'

'Marlene Dietrich,' she said again.

During rehearsals of *Something in the Air*, Marlene and the smallish, quietly charming young composer were to establish a lifelong friendship. Spoliansky had written a duet for two girls, for which Marlene was teamed with a well-known revue artist, Margo Lion. Their number was one of the hits of the show, and also required both of them to display their legs as well as their talents. Dietrich's legs undoubtedly won.

The revue ran for several months at the Komoedie, and during this time Marlene's life seemed to become more measured and settled. She went rarely to parties now, and whenever she did, she was asked to sing. *I'd like to be a little happy* was one of her favourite numbers, *but if I were too happy, I'd miss being sad . . .*

She lavished affection on her daughter, calling her *Heideke* and extolling her perfection to friends. When she and Rudolph moved to a bigger flat, to 54 Kaiser Allee, Wilmersdorf, not far from the house in which she had lived as a child, its largest and most important room was the nursery.

After *Something in the Air*, Reinhardt cast Marlene as a rich and glamorous American woman in his next production, a musical play by George Kaiser, *Zwei Kravatten*, for which Spoliansky again wrote the score. It opened to an enthusiastic Press, and Marlene was especially praised.

One night during the run a sharp-featured, short, and thick-set man with a rather Mephistophelean moustache was in the audience. He had come for a special reason. He had heard about Marlene Dietrich, although he was in search of something that he was fast beginning to believe did not exist.

CHAPTER EIGHT

The Blue Angel

The man who came to the Komoedie Theatre that night, and who was to exert so powerful an influence over the future of Marlene Dietrich, was Josef von Sternberg. Born thirty-six years previously in Vienna, of Polish and Hungarian parents, he had gone to America with his family at the age of seven, and by 1914 was working in New York—for Hollywood was not yet the centre of American film production—as an assistant cutter. Ten years later, having gained technical experience in a variety of jobs, he managed to raise a few thousand dollars to make an independent film.

The Salvation Hunters, a story of down-and-outs in a little community on the California coast, was released early in 1925 and met with considerable critical success. It also attracted the attention of influential people, notably Charles Chaplin—who was later to use the leading actress, Georgia Hale, as the heroine of *The Gold Rush*—and Mary Pickford, who commissioned von Sternberg to write a story for her. Later, however, they disagreed and the project was abandoned; and von Sternberg's uncompromising independence and dominating personality was, in fact, to involve him in a series of disagreements with the producers who employed him over the next few years. It was not until 1927 that he made a film which both pleased the critics and restored Hollywood's confidence in him. The success of *Underworld*, a gangster film, was followed by *The Docks of New York*, a low-life story, and *The Last Command*, about the life of a Hollywood extra, played by Emil Jannings.

Jannings returned to Germany soon after making this film, but early in 1930 sent von Sternberg a copy of *Professor Unrath* by Heinrich Mann. This novel described the fatal passion of a middle-aged professor for a beautiful but sluttish cabaret singer, Lola-Lola Frolich, unofficial agent for a group of politicians identified in all but name with the Nazis. For her sake the professor not only endured personal humiliation, but allowed himself to be used by Lola-Lola's political friends. Von Sternberg liked the subject, and Eric Pommer of UFA agreed to produce it. But it was now 1930, and the imminence of the Nazis' rise to power could be felt; von Sternberg decided to omit the political element of the story and make sexual domination the reason for the professor's downfall. Lola-Lola was to be a modern *femme fatale*, sexuality incarnate.

Only one difficulty remained: to find the actress to play Lola-Lola. Pommer wanted Lucie Mannheim for the part, but von Sternberg was dissatisfied with her test. More than twenty other actresses were tested, but none fitted the director's conception of the character. Von Sternberg was less concerned to find an actress than a girl of extreme physical beauty, with the kind of calculated glamour that alone could make the story convincing. He was in search of a great temptress.

When he saw Marlene Dietrich in *Zwei Kravatten* he knew his search had ended.

After the show, von Sternberg went round to Marlene's dressing-room and introduced himself. He described the film and the part, and told her he was convinced that only she could play Lola-Lola. But Marlene was doubtful. She told him that she wasn't good in films, she photographed badly, she didn't feel she could do it.

Von Sternberg was unmoved by this. 'You *have* to play it,' he said, then made a little bow and wished her good night.

Next morning he telephoned her. He told her he had arranged

a test for the following day, and she was to learn a 'vulgar' song.

Marlene did not learn a song, but she arrived for the test. ('Inquisitive and a little afraid,' she remembers.) She sang one of her favourite American numbers, *You're the cream in my coffee*, and when the test was over he walked across and held out his hands. 'You have a beautiful face which lives—really lives,' he said.

A few days later Marlene signed the contract, and *The Blue Angel*, as it was to be called, went into production.

The Blue Angel, of course, is part of film history, both for itself and for its creation of the Dietrich myth. Von Sternberg worked assiduously to capture in Lola-Lola the image of a classic temptress; he bathed Dietrich in an unrelenting erotic atmosphere, to which everything—costume, lighting, backgrounds, camera-angles —contributed. Perhaps no other film has contained such concentrated sexual imagery and implication. Sometimes the ugly realism of a setting—a shabby, untidy little dressing-room with its make-up jars and powder puffs everywhere—was used to counterpoint Lola-Lola's beauty. Sometimes, as she stood with one leg resting on a chair, the camera moved in to emphasise the black-stockinged thigh, with its frilly garter, in the foreground of the composition. Most memorable of all was Lola-Lola on the cabaret stage, with its backcloth of a harbour, its clutter of birds and caryatids, its smoky lighting; in her high heels and black silk tights, plumes waving round her neck and, perversely, a silk top hat on her head, she sang one of Friedrich Hollander's songs in a tired, deliberately monotonous voice:

> *Falling in love again,*
> *Never wanted to.*
> *What am I to do?*
> *I can't help it . . .*

The collaboration between director and star was very close. It was evident on the set that Dietrich had unlimited respect for von

Sternberg as an artist, and made her creative will complementary to his own. At times, Jannings—who, like Pommer, had at first opposed the casting of Dietrich—was clearly jealous of the care and attention she received. When it came to shooting the scene in which the Professor attacks Lola-Lola and tries to strangle her, the passionate realism of Jannings' acting was unmistakable. Marlene described it later:

'Jannings really seemed to want to strangle me. My throat was black and blue for days after the scene was shot . . .'

When von Sternberg saw the rough-cut of *The Blue Angel*, he was certain he had made the discovery of a lifetime; and the personality that was to emerge from this film—aloof, languorous, faintly cruel—was very different from the Marlene Dietrich of the Berlin stage.

He sent an enthusiastic telegram about her to B P Schulberg, executive producer for Paramount Pictures in Hollywood.

CHAPTER NINE

Hollywood

It was the right moment to arouse Schulberg's interest, because this was the time of an invasion of Hollywood by foreign stars. It had started, of course, when Mauritz Stiller brought Greta Garbo across from Sweden, and MGM signed her to an exclusive contract. Every studio hoped to discover a Garbo now. Schulberg had at least secured Maurice Chevalier for Paramount; and his appetite was whetted. He asked von Sternberg to return as soon as *The Blue Angel* was finished, and to bring a copy of it with him.

Von Sternberg sailed to America a few weeks later, and Schulberg, with a group of studio executives, technicians and publicists, saw the film in a private projection theatre. Their verdict was unanimous—'Sign Dietrich'. The studio contacted its representative in Berlin, and also sent an offer by cable direct to Dietrich.

When the Paramount representative called on Dietrich in Berlin, she seemed unperturbed. He asked her if she had received the cable. 'Yes, I have,' she answered quite simply. He asked her why she hadn't answered it. 'I don't want to go to America,' she said.

The usual promises followed—she would be rich, she would be famous, and she would only have to sign a contract for six months. Marlene pointed out that she already had a contract in Berlin, but the representative said that Paramount would buy her out of it. When she still hesitated, he brought out his trump card. Von Sternberg was on his way to fetch her.

'When must I go if I sign?' she asked.

In a matter of days, the representative told her, as they had a film ready to start shooting in a few weeks.

Overpowered as she was by her first encounter with Hollywood methods, it was not this which determined Marlene to sign the contract. It was the knowledge that von Sternberg wanted her.

Schulberg was told of her decision by cable, and gave orders for *The Blue Angel*, as soon as final prints were ready, to be booked on the Paramount circuit in America. A few days later von Sternberg arrived in Berlin to collect his *protegée*, with the script of *Morocco* under his arm.

'The only way to succeed,' von Sternberg was reported to have said once, 'is by making people hate you.' With Marlene Dietrich, however, this was certainly not his method. Not only had she found in him a director and an artist whom she enormously admired, to whose creative drive and understanding she responded, but for von Sternberg himself Dietrich had become an obsession —an obsession in which the actress could not be separated from the woman. Later, this was to cause a good deal of unfounded Hollywood gossip, aided no doubt by the fact that though von Sternberg was married his wife remained in the background of his professional life, and that Marlene arrived in America without Rudolph. It was, in fact, the true professional relationship that Hollywood could never understand; and because of this, von Sternberg and Dietrich were surrounded by speculation and inference.

Rudolph arranged to follow her shortly. Marlene said a sad goodbye to little Maria; it was clear the child would miss her. Nor, as she wondered about the future on board the *Bremen*, were these her only regrets. Von Sternberg was there to give her confidence, but she felt she might be lonely, and she was unnerved by the suddenness with which everything had happened.

The Hollywood in which she arrived was still in a mood of

extravagance only slightly less marked than that of the twenties. The arrival of the talkies had averted a slump that was impending three years earlier, and a revived confidence was in the air; new talent was coming in from Broadway and Europe, and old talent, unable to make the transition from silence to sound, was failing. It was the year of the great D W Griffith's last film, *Abraham Lincoln*. It was the year of *All Quiet on the Western Front*, of Garbo's *Anna Christie* and the Marx Brothers' *Monkey Business* and Wallace Beery in *The Big House*. The big stars were Chaplin, Garbo, Gloria Swanson, John Barrymore, Clara Bow, Chevalier, Norma Shearer, Jeannette Macdonald. If the great legendary symbols—the prize Borzois, the caged panther in the garden, the Beauvais tapestry in the entrance hall—were a little less in evidence now, Hollywood was still an extraordinary and feverish place.

The arrival of actress and director in the land of dreams was not, however, attended by great publicity. Paramount had decided to be cunning, and reveal Dietrich later, as a 'surprise'. A few days after she had settled in and started preparatory work with von Sternberg on *Morocco*, a few papers reported that the director had returned with a new 'discovery'; a few speculations were released when they were seen lunching together at a restaurant, and then the subject—for lack of information—was dropped.

The shooting of *Morocco* was uneventful, mainly because Paramount had decided to delay its publicity campaign. One or two incidents, however, reached the limelight. In this story of a cabaret singer who falls in love with a Foreign Legionnaire, Dietrich played opposite a rising young star, Gary Cooper. Cooper was then married to the Mexican actress Lupe Velez. The fact that Marlene and her leading man got on well together and became friends was enough, apparently, to inflame Cooper's wife with jealousy and inspire her to the kind of public pronouncement for which she had a taste. This time she was recorded as saying she would 'tear Marlene Dietrich's eyes out'—if she ever came within reach of them, which history records, fortunately, she did not. Similarly, the fact that Marlene was only seen in public with von Sternberg, renewed the usual rumours and queries. Public speculation of this kind is one of the extraordinary facts of Hollywood life.

A good illustration, in a different vein, of the fact behind fantasy, was given by Leonard Lyons, who tells a story about Marlene's first day on the set of *Morocco*. Von Sternberg had apparently put his new star through a scene no less than a dozen times, although all she had to do was to walk through a doorway and then turn round. There was to be a big close-up of her standing in the doorway, and von Sternberg told her to count three to herself before she turned. When they tried it again, he told her to count six, then ten, and finally twenty. In this important moment of the film, a critic later remarked, one could see in Dietrich's eyes a fear and a realisation of the years of tragedy ahead. 'What I was actually thinking to myself at the time,' Marlene confessed afterwards, 'was that if this is the way pictures are made here, I'm taking the first boat home tomorrow . . .'

The technicians working on *Morocco* found the new star refreshingly courteous and untemperamental; the property man, in fact, christened her 'The Pink Angel'. As before, she worked closely and devotedly with von Sternberg. *Morocco* was a highly artificial romantic picture, taking place in an elegantly sordid corner of the East. The director lavished upon it all his characteristic effects of lighting and design, and introduced what was to become one of his favourite pictorial devices—the use of slatted shutters, through which much of the action was seen, to cast long striped shadows in the littered, dusty interiors, and across the narrow spidery

47

streets of the studio-built Moroccan town. (Some years later, when von Sternberg was introduced to the Pasha of Marrakesh in the South of France, El Glaoui asked him what locations in Morocco he used for the film. Von Sternberg told him calmly that the entire film had been shot in California and he had never been to Morocco in his life.) The whole atmosphere of the film was deliberately languid and decadent, and Dietrich had several sophisticated numbers to sing. At least one of them, for which she wore a white tuxedo and top hat, contained some specialised sexual allusions that would almost certainly not be passed by the censor today.

By the time shooting was finished, Marlene was homesick. Rudolph had not been able to follow her out, and though of course they wrote to each other frequently—Marlene's letters were full of anxious enquiries about Maria—she was feeling lonely and unsettled. She had been installed with the usual Hollywood comfort—a pleasant house, a maid and two servants and a Rolls Royce supplied by Paramount—but she did not care for Hollywood social life. Her spare time was spent in an occasional visit to boxing matches and football games, and in the company of von Sternberg.

She was bored, too, by the constant comparisons drawn between herself and Garbo. These were inspired, no doubt, by her relative withdrawal from social life and the fact that the studio enjoyed making a mystery of her. Once she made an unsuccessful protest. 'She must think I am trying to imitate her,' a journalist reported her as saying. 'But there is nobody like Garbo. I am new to the screen, but I think she is the greatest star in the world.'

When Garbo's attention was drawn to this praise, she made no comment. She only asked politely: 'And who is Marlene Dietrich?'

CHAPTER TEN

Return to Berlin

When von Sternberg showed the rough-cut of *Morocco* to the Paramount executives, however, they were convinced that 'the new Garbo' had arrived. The label stuck, and one magazine even opened a referendum: *'Who will be the great star of tomorrow—Garbo or Dietrich?'*

A journalist who interviewed her at this time described the new star as wearing a somewhat masculine outfit—slacks and a well-cut jacket; and a soft felt hat, almost trilby in shape, on the seat beside her. She told him she was unhappy in Hollywood, and had begun to wonder if it was a mistake to have come. As for fame, she preferred the company of her little daughter in Berlin.

When Sam Goldwyn read this article, another writer alleged, he chuckled and suggested that Marlene was trying to imitate Garbo . . .

'Marlene,' another journalist wrote after interviewing her, 'has a round face, a turned-up nose, she is more humanly pretty than Greta Garbo because she knows how to smile. She is more humble than the disdainful Garbo, but, like Garbo, she is unhappy in America when not working. She stays at home, reading, or thinking about her young husband who is working in films in Germany, or about her baby, whom she adores, and whose photos she takes everywhere with her.'

All of this happened to be true. Off the set, Marlene was usually melancholy; she preferred the quiet of her home to Hollywood night life, and she thought a great deal about Rudolph and Maria.

Mother and daughter even exchanged frequent recordings of their voices.

In spite of all this, her allegiance to von Sternberg remained unshaken. When Paramount, on the strength of the *Morocco* rough-cut, offered her a new contract, she accepted but insisted on the additional clause that only von Sternberg should direct her pictures.

As with *The Blue Angel*, their collaboration extended to the final cutting of the film. (Von Sternberg has more than once acknowledged Marlene's technical grasp of film-making, and the helpfulness of her advice at this stage.) A few days after it was finished, he told her he was about to begin work on a new story for her.

Marlene, however, was adamant about one thing. Before she started work again, she was going home to see her daughter. She had, in fact, already booked a passage from New York.

Von Sternberg agreed, and told her he would join her in Berlin within three weeks.

Rudolph and Maria, and Gerda Huber, were at the station to meet Marlene when her train arrived in Berlin. There were also large crowds, for *The Blue Angel* had been playing to packed houses and Marlene was already a celebrity in Europe. Gerda has since described the scene:

'It was our own Marlene coming back, and she looked like a convalescent after a long and serious illness. It may sound odd, but that was the impression Rudolph and I had of her. She was no longer beautiful—in fact, she seemed almost plain. Her cheeks were hollow, her eyes looked sunken without their artificial shadow, and they had nothing of the serenity and brilliance we remembered. But her smile and her voice were unchanged. Her slender figure was wrapped in a chinchilla cloak, and almost hidden by a bouquet of orchids. Police were obliged to restrain the crowds, but she seemed unconscious of their presence.'

After the first embraces, Maria demanded the electric toy motor car she had been promised. That evening, when Marlene was back in her home, she was clearly overjoyed. Gerda, who was invited to supper, remembers Rudolph asking for his favourite pistachio ice cream; and Marlene at once put on her apron and started to make it. For the next fortnight she threw herself into being a wife and mother, and wanted nothing else. Hollywood might never have existed.

'I have visited her in her daughter's playroom,' a German journalist wrote, 'surrounded by a doll's house, a cot, a doll's pram and a toy shop. I have seen what could be a charming scene in a film—a young mother welcomes home her daughter after an outing: as she takes off the little girl's out-door clothes, she quickly imprints a kiss on every available piece of bare flesh. It was then that I saw Marlene as her acting career has never revealed her. It may be fate or it may be simply part of the job that obliges film stars to be identified with their roles off-screen. But Dietrich is different. She reacts to beauty, and for her beauty is within her child. While Maria played, Marlene Dietrich said to me: "If you think it right to tell people something of my personal life, please say," and she pointed to her daughter, "please say *that* is the most important thing in it. I am content—work has always been exciting and has sometimes made me happy, but fame has nothing to do with real happiness. The longing continues in spite of fame . . ."'

One is reminded of what Milton Shulman wrote in the London *Evening Standard* some years ago, when Marlene returned for a season at the Café de Paris. 'In every *femme fatale* there is a *Hausfrau* trying to get out . . .'

For while Marlene played with her daughter and cooked for Rudolph, *The Blue Angel* opened in America and enjoyed a tremendous success, and pictures of the star in smart male attire appeared everywhere.

Rudolph's contract in Berlin was due to expire soon, and then he would be free to go to Hollywood and join his wife when she started work on her new film. Meanwhile, he would not accept a penny from her; he considered himself responsible for his own living, and for supporting Maria.

After fifteen days von Sternberg arrived in Berlin, as he had promised. He went to see Marlene with the script of his new story for her, *Dishonoured.* 'Once again,' Gerda Huber later recalled, 'once again Marlene came completely under his spell . . .'

CHAPTER ELEVEN

The Legend

'Josef,' Marlene Dietrich said, 'there's simply one thing I must have in *Dishonoured*. I must have a cat in it—cats always bring me luck.'

Back in Hollywood, actress and director were preparing their new film in an atmosphere of even greater seclusion than usual. Von Sternberg issued a new edict: no interviews to be given by Dietrich unless he personally had given permission for them, and no Press stories to be released by the publicity department without his approval. He had insisted, too, that he and Marlene must work together alone, and it was arranged that Rudolph and Maria should not join her until the end of shooting, in about three months' time.

Gerda went to Hollywood with Marlene, however, as secretary-companion.

While they worked, *Morocco* opened to a flamboyant publicity campaign. In those days, aeroplanes emblazoned with the star's name in enormous letters still flew low over New York and other big cities for such occasions. Not that they were really needed to make the world Dietrich-conscious; the Press, with an endless series of photographs and gossip, and the gramophone record sales of her songs from *The Blue Angel*, were already doing more than enough.

It was evident that von Sternberg intended *Dishonoured*, a spy story set in Vienna with Marlene as a secret agent disguised as a prostitute, to repeat the opulent pictorial style, the artificial settings and lighting effects, the elaborate costumes, of the previous film. He engaged the same cameraman and set designer, and discussed at length with Marlene the details of a particularly languorous creation covered with black sequins.

Marlene's new leading man, playing a Russian spy, was Victor MacLaglen, the huge and genial son of an English clergyman who had been a boxer before turning to films and becoming a star in Hollywood after *The Beloved Brute* and *What Price Glory*. Noted for his equable and easy-going disposition, he must have felt something of an outsider on the *Dishonoured* set. Once again von Sternberg and Dietrich worked together with complete concentration, discussing the lighting of a close-up, the adjustment of a veil, the exact gesture of rouging her lips. Very often, in the interpretation of a scene, there seemed to exist between them an almost unspoken understanding; she seemed to know instinctively what he wanted. Occasionally von Sternberg flew into a rage, but Marlene seemed to appreciate his rages. 'To look at those two,' MacLaglen was heard to comment once, 'gives me a temperature . . .'

When shooting was finished, Marlene decided to return at once to Berlin to collect Rudolph and Maria. Von Sternberg was unhappy about this, because he wanted her to stay and work with him on the cutting of the picture. 'It has been my greatest regret,' he said in an interview to a young female journalist, 'that Marlene left for Germany before *Dishonoured* was cut. It would have been a much finer picture if she had been in the cutting-room working with me, as she did on *Morocco* and *The Blue Angel*. She has a sixth sense for cutting.'

The director's adulation of her did not end there. The interviewer disclosed that she had recently been questioning von Sternberg's script-girl, who had worked on both Marlene's Hollywood films.

'What did you find out?' von Sternberg asked her. 'Did she

share the unanimous opinion that Miss Dietrich is probably the most fascinating actress she has ever seen? Did she tell you that everyone on the set loved her, and that her greatest tribulation had been that Miss Dietrich would never appear with her hair done the same way more than once? Did the script-girl tell you how she stood to one side and wrung her hands with consternation when, according to her continuity notes, Miss Dietrich sat at the piano in the jail scene in *Dishonoured*, her hair parted on the right side—and how in the next shot it was parted directly in the middle?

'Did she tell you how, later in the same sequence, Miss Dietrich ran her fingers through her hair, and there was no parting visible at all? And how, when it was called to Miss Dietrich's attention, she laughed and said, "What does it matter? This is the way I wear it now".'

The interview seems to have been conducted in a genial mood, and finished with von Sternberg inviting the girl to dinner with himself and Marlene when she returned.

Meanwhile, during her absence, the director was more loquacious than usual to the Press. Perhaps he was trying to dissipate the impression of exclusiveness and secret domination, the rumours that Dietrich was not allowed to smile all part of a legend that had undoubtedly captured public imagination.

'Marlene Dietrich is the most intelligent woman I have ever known, and the most thoughtful,' he remarked to another journalist. 'The moment I saw her playing on the stage in Berlin, I knew at once I wanted her for my picture. There was apparent in her a strange mixture of worldly sophistication and cultured refinement. She carried the illusion of perfect indifference . . .

'She is the most thoughtful person I have ever met in my life. If I put my hand out for some paper in order to write down notes, and there is no paper there, the next day I will find a silver tablet and a pencil on the arm of my chair. Nothing is ever said about it. Marlene has the feeling that there is nothing so important as the thing we are working upon. When I am directing a picture, building it up step by step, her one desire seems to be that every need of mine should be anticipated—every irritation removed. Why, she even thinks about the most healthful food I should eat.'

Marlene, he continued, would prepare special German dishes that she knew he liked, and send her maid to the studio with them. Her intelligence, brilliant though it was, in no way detracted from her quality of being the most feminine woman he had ever known. As an actress she was a perfectionist, and she understood camera angles almost as well as the man operating the camera.

Marlene had returned to Berlin with the present of a terrier for Maria, and was arranging the details of Rudolph's and her daughter's move to Hollywood. She found that a fashion she had already started in America was now spreading to Europe: her severely cut masculine jackets and slacks were being copied everywhere, and slouch, soft felt hats designed on the style of the Englishman's trilby. Women were even ordering shirts from male outfitters with male ties to match, and the ensemble was known as 'The Dietrich Style'. Marlene herself, when questioned on the subject, merely remarked, 'I wear these clothes because they are comfortable,' and smiled.

But the Berlin to which she came back had also changed in a more profound way. This was 1932, and the imminence of the New Order, of the Nazi party, was unmistakable. Marlene went to a big fancy dress ball in top hat and tails; also at the ball were Party members, uniformed and jackbooted, and not in fancy dress. They were becoming familiar sights at many social occasions, at theatres and night clubs. The first anti-Jewish slogans, also, were appearing, and Walter Rilla, with whom Marlene had filmed in the twenties, went to a theatre one night and found a notice,

'Jews Prohibited', chalked up beside the stage door. When he protested, the theatre director explained that his assistant stage manager was a Party member, and he was frightened of reprisals if the notice were taken down. It was not long after this that Rilla decided to leave Germany.

During this return visit, Marlene was often seen in the company of a new friend, Hans Jaray, then an unknown young actor, but later to become famous in his own light comedies which were to earn him the description of 'the Noël Coward of Berlin'. Many people believe today that it was Dietrich's interest in him that helped Jaray to develop his talent. Throughout her life, in fact, she was to show an almost uncanny sense for discovering talent and supporting it with wise advice and practical help.

When Marlene returned to her Beverly Hills home this time, Rudolph and Maria came with her. They arrived shortly after the opening of *Dishonoured*, which proved another personal success for the star. The film itself carried von Sternberg's pictorial aestheticism a stage further, and as melodrama it was rather slow and heavy, almost abstract at times; the chief impression was of a series of beautifully lit, cluttered sets and a strong emphasis on costume—Marlene was swathed in furs, covered in sequins, draped in seductive veiling, and never looked less than wonderfully beautiful and mysterious even if, in addition to her prostitute disguise, the plot also required her to appear as a peasant woman, without make-up and to be practically invisible inside a heavy flying suit. That it intensified the *femme fatale* legend, however, there can be no doubt. A tribute paid by C H Rand, a well-known journalist of the time, was typical:

'I would cheerfully walk ten miles to see a film that had Marlene Dietrich in it, or motor five hundred miles through snow. I know well enough, of course, that the enchantment is not Marlene alone. I see her through the eyes of cunning artists. I see her through the eyes of Josef von Sternberg. I see her through the eyes of her talented cameramen, art directors and dress designers. I see her in shot after shot of almost too perfect composition until she moves in a world of her own . . . Like all the great film characters, Marlene is a myth, a symbol, an idea. And it is because she is the perfect embodiment of that idea that she has this fascination for me. As with all men, a fair part of my subconscious life spends itself in a dream of a perfect vamp. Your Latin or Slav vamps of the Pola Negri type don't happen to interest me. I want beauty without bust-ups; temptation without temperament. I want a woman whose passion is not a blind rage of the body or the soul, but a recognition of mutual attraction in which reason or humour will play their part, as far as love permits. But vamps with brains are far to seek. And vamps with humour even further. I find all my requisites in the screen character of Marlene Dietrich. She has beauty in abundance. She has a rich, sensuous allure. And you have only to look at her eyes to see that she has brains, and at her mouth to see that she has humour.'

Nor was this all that Mr Rand saw in Marlene Dietrich. He rated her brains on a par with such dominating personalities as Napoleon, Caesar, Mussolini and Lenin. If you ever bargained with her, she would always be two moves ahead. If you thought her aloof, this was only because you recognised her superiority. She had no illusions about love only because she was too wise for them . . .

It had, certainly, become a legend to live up to.

CHAPTER TWELVE

Settled out of Court

When Marlene started work with von Sternberg on her third
Hollywood picture, *Shanghai Express*, Rudolph and Maria were
with her at the house in Beverly Hills, as well as Gerda and two
maidservants brought from Berlin. In spite of this, the buzzing
rumours concerning the actress and her director showed no signs
of abating—though Rudolph was apparently unperturbed by
them. In his eyes, there was merely an unusually close professional relationship between his wife and von Sternberg, of which
the films were proof. He did not regard the director's influence
as in any way sinister.

Hollywood, however, persisted in doing so. The fact that Marlene's life was now divided between her family and her work
meant that she was seldom seen on social occasions, or taking
part in the film city's night-life.

Rumours were also circulating that Marlene wanted to break
away from von Sternberg and work with a new director. This she
also denied. 'Before I had my child,' she said, 'I stopped and
looked at every child in the street, I was so crazy about all children. But now, when I have my own child, that is perfection.
Why should I look at others? I feel that way about directors. I
have the best—why should I look at others?'

And, to the inevitable suggestions that her marriage was not
all it appeared to be, Dietrich quietly explained that one should
look for something beyond appearances. No two marriages ever
looked alike, but all that mattered was how a marriage looked to

the people involved. 'When two people love one another, they should know how it is between them. I haven't a strong sense of possession towards a man. Maybe that's because I am not particularly feminine in my reactions. I never have been. Even when I was younger I didn't want to attract boys—in fact, I very much wanted not to attract them. I had no *beaux*, no crushes, till I met my husband.'

Marlene, it was clear, was as much of an individualist as her director, and Hollywood was finding her equally difficult to understand. Not that it seemed to worry her. The production of *Shanghai Express*, a melodrama in which Dietrich played Shanghai Lily, a white prostitute who found herself in much the same situation as Boule de Suif when the train on which she was travelling was attacked by revolutionaries, proceeded to the usual plan. Long and intimate conferences between director and star on lighting, on costumes, on the most detailed points of interpretation: and plenty of cluttered, exquisitely photographed sets—mainly sinister Oriental interiors this time, draped in net and bamboo.

However much Dietrich and von Sternberg were prepared to ignore the gossip-mongers, there was a limit, apparently, to what the director's wife could stand. As *Shanghai Express* finished shooting, Mrs Risa Royce von Sternberg divorced her husband and announced she was suing Marlene Dietrich for £100,000 damages for alienation of her husband's affections, and for a further £20,000 for alleged libel. The threatened action was of course reported in the newspapers the world over. The director's wife was interviewed by correspondents and gave them details of the grievances which she believed she had against Miss Dietrich. Mrs von Sternberg had, she said, been a 'faithful loving wife for four years . . .'

The libel, Mrs von Sternberg explained, appeared in an article attributed to Marlene in an American magazine. (In actual fact this article was a reprint of one written by a certain Dr Sandor Incze in Vienna, slanted to the usual Trilby-Svengali theme.) According to this article, Marlene had remarked some time ago that von Sternberg was going to divorce his wife because she made him unhappy.

Nor could Mrs von Sternberg resist telling the *Daily Mail* reporter what she thought of Dietrich. 'Any woman who lowers her voice and talks in whispers and looks out of the corners of her eyes can get a reputation for being mysterious. I could myself, if I tried . . .'

A few days later, the London *Daily Mail* reported Marlene as saying: 'Rudolph and I love each other, and together we will fight the lawsuits.' Other newspapers, naturally, made all the headlines they could out of the situation, and claimed to have extracted similar statements from the star. Out of all this, two facts emerged. One was that Dietrich had actually been served with the legal papers several months previously, but the suits had not yet been filed in New York; the other was that von Sternberg had been urging his wife to abandon the actions and had promised to assume full financial responsibility.

Then Marlene announced that she was not prepared to consider any financial settlement out of court. However much publicity might be involved, she would contest all Mrs von Sternberg's charges, which were unsubstantiated and untrue. Rudolph was also reported as having issued a statement to the same effect.

In two weeks it was all over. Paramount studios put an end to speculation by announcing that Marlene had received a letter from Mrs von Sternberg, informing her that she had dropped the suit after discovering that the evidence on which she had based her allegations was false. Dr Incze, whose original article had caused so much trouble, published a statement that his report of Marlene's remark about Mrs von Sternberg had 'absolutely no foundation in fact.'

What the London *Daily Express* hopefully described as a 'first-class triangle sensation' never reached the courts. After a great deal of speculation, the 'sensation', in fact, dwindled to an amiable anticlimax, and apart from the divorce itself, Hollywood felt that it really knew no more than it had before.

CHAPTER THIRTEEN

Von for All

'Do you think,' Gerda asked Marlene one evening, as they sat with Rudolph in her drawing-room, 'that Josef has got over his fascination for you?'

Marlene's eyes, according to Gerda, became inscrutable. 'I don't know,' she said, 'I don't know. When we are in the studio together, I am overcome by delight in my work, I feel that without him I should be absolutely nothing. I am his creature—and he is the one and only man who is capable of bringing out my true self.'

'The self,' Rudolph interjected quickly, 'that is a born mother.'

Perhaps Rudolph knew something already of the subject of Marlene's next film for von Sternberg, *Blonde Venus*—he could hardly have been referring to Marlene's characterisations in *The Blue Angel* or *Shanghai Express*. The story of *Blonde Venus* was what is popularly known as a 'weepie'. It concerned a cabaret singer who, in order to raise money to help her seriously ill husband, became the mistress of a rich man-about-town. When the husband discovered this, he threatened to deprive her of her child. She took the child away from him, wandering from city to city, first as an entertainer, finally as a prostitute. Unable to bring up her daughter properly any more, she sent her back to her husband. Shortly after this she became a music-hall sensation in Paris, as a result of which she was reunited with husband and child.

While they worked together on the script of *Blonde Venus*, according to Gerda, Marlene was moved to tears. Once she took

63

von Sternberg's hand, raised it to her lips and said: 'I hope I shall never fail you.'

Blonde Venus was cast—with Herbert Marshall as the husband and Cary Grant as the rich lover—and ready to go into production when Schulberg and the other Paramount executives summoned von Sternberg to a conference and informed him that they considered the ending 'immoral'. American audiences, they felt, would not accept the final scene of a husband forgiving a wife who had so degraded herself.

Von Sternberg, however, refused to change the ending and was characteristically uncompromising about it. The result was a threat from the studio to cancel his contract and give Marlene a new director, Richard Wallace.

Marlene herself was at the conference, and had not spoken a word during the argument. But now she rose from her chair and quietly remarked that if Paramount cancelled von Sternberg's contract it would have to cancel her own as well. 'I will never,' she said, 'accept another director.'

Von Sternberg now tried to dissuade her, but she merely took his arm and moved towards the door. 'Let's go,' she said, 'it's useless to discuss it any further,' and led him out of the office.

Battle had been joined, and for a few days the outcome was uncertain. Rudolph supported Marlene and her director, and the Hollywood colony quickly christened the trio 'The Three Musketeers'. Marlene, going one better, coined the slogan:

'Von for all and all for von!'

Paramount's next move was to stop Marlene's pay. This drew no reaction from her, and for a month the deadlock continued. Then von Sternberg decided it was up to him to make a gesture. He told Marlene that they must not risk ruining her career, and went to see the Paramount executives. As a result, a small and unimportant modification was introduced into the plot of *Blonde*

Before *The Blue Angel*

At the time of *The Blue Angel*

In *The Blue Angel* (*below* with Emil Jannings)

In *The Blue Angel*

In *Three Loves* (with Fritz Kortner)

In Hollywood

With Sir Harry Lauder and Ernest Lubitsch

Above: In *Dishonoured*
Below: In *The Devil Is A Woman*

Above: With Charlie Chaplin

Below left: With von Sternberg

Below right: With Maurice Chevalier

Above: In *Morocco*
Below: In *Blonde Venus* (with Cary Grant)

Above left: Early Hollywood portrait   *Above right:* In *Stage Fright*
Below left: In *Kismet*   *Below right:* In *Knight Without Armour*

With Rudolph Sieber (on left) and others at time of *Morocco*

In *Shanghai Express* with Anna May Wong and Warner Oland

An early Hollywood portrait

Mother and daughter in *The Scarlet Empress*

Above: After the fight scene in *Destry Rides Again*
Below: In *A Foreign Affair*

Venus, and all parties announced that they had reached agreement—albeit a temporary agreement.

When the film started shooting, the strain of Hollywood was beginning to show in von Sternberg. He was already thinking about his next film with Marlene—she had acquired a story in Europe during her last holiday, and asked him to consider it. One day he said to a reporter:

'I think I'll go sick on this next picture and stay away two weeks and let Marlene direct it. After all, she almost directed *Morocco* and *Dishonoured*. I mean it.'

When a magazine writer suggested that Dietrich was 'a parrot', he said: 'I am going to make very few more pictures. I am going to retire. I have few more stories left in me and I am going to take a long rest. I shall recommend that Marlene direct them. A parrot? Why, she spent hours every day in Europe hunting for stories, not only for herself but for Paramount to produce with other players. The only thing I put into her mouth is good English.'

It was said that von Sternberg's criticisms of Marlene's English at this time were so harsh that she would ironically retaliate by firing questions at him in German.

At this time, too, an incident occurred that emphasised one of Marlene's most persistent traits—her generosity. One of the many struggling aspirants to stardom in Hollywood was a twenty-six-year-old man from Scotland, who had resigned his commission in the army, because he found peace-time soldiering dull, and gone to Canada. There he had worked on a newspaper, as a waiter and a lumberjack; plantation work in Cuba attracted him next, then a revolution in Peru. When the adventurous young Scotsman turned up in Hollywood to try his luck, he found it difficult at first. One incident from his early days has remained in his mind.

'When I first arrived,' he has said, 'I knew nobody in the film world and I had never acted in my life. Consequently I sat around for quite a long time looking hopeful but getting more broke by the minute. Marlene was then the glamour queen, and was driven around in the biggest private automobile ever built. Her chauffeur, named Briggs, had two revolvers strapped to his legs and a splendid jacket with a mink collar draped about his shoulders. I was lucky enough to meet Marlene at a party and, of course, have loved her deeply and devotedly ever since. Once in those early days I got ill. I got 'flu or something. I was living in a room over a garage in Hollywood, and I was now broke and very miserable. At my lowest ebb, the biggest automobile ever built suddenly glided up and Briggs came staggering into the room carrying food and medicine and champagne and caviar, and even a huge cake which Marlene had made herself. She happens to be a sensational cook, too.

'That was a typical act of impulsive kindness and generosity—she had heard that someone she hardly knew was ill and lonely and miserable, and she reacted in what I now know to be typical Dietrich fashion.'

A few years later the young man, whose name was David Niven, got his first part in *Rose Marie,* and quickly became a star.

Rudolph had now been appointed the Paramount representative in Berlin, which involved spending several months of the year in Europe and making twice-yearly visits to his wife. As *Blonde Venus* finished shooting he left for Berlin, and von Sternberg left for the West Indies with a cameraman, Paul Ivano, to gather background for a circus story in which he proposed to star Dietrich. He was mainly in search of a hurricane, which obstinately refused to materialise. He grew tired of waiting and decided to go off on a long holiday to Europe.

Marlene decided that she did not want to remain alone in Hollywood, and she sailed to join Rudolph in Berlin. Before she left, a reporter asked her if she felt that Hollywood had changed her.

'I do not believe I have changed,' she said, 'except to grow a little older. And I have more responsibilities. When one makes a picture, one feels that a whole production rests on one's shoulders. But Hollywood? It doesn't do anything drastic to people— certainly not to people with strong personalities and minds of their own.'

Inevitably, the same old theory was brought up again. 'Anyone with intelligence,' she answered, 'can see that I'm not hypnotised. Obviously I have something of my own behind my face. You can't put a brain into a woman's head if it isn't there already . . .'

Blonde Venus was not quite the success Marlene and her director had hoped it would be. Nor did it make the sort of money that Paramount had expected it to make. It had its surprising moments—notably when Marlene sang *Hot Voodoo* in a fuzzy blonde wig and an ape-skin—but it seemed that the public and the critics were growing a little weary of the studied unreality of von Sternberg's pictures. They were agreed on one thing only: that Marlene looked more beautiful than ever.

CHAPTER FOURTEEN

Ordeal

On her return to America, Marlene Dietrich was to undergo a frightening ordeal. It began, curiously enough, on Friday the 13th —of May 1932.

Not long before this date, the newspapers had been full of the kidnapping of Colonel Lindbergh's child. After weeks of intensive police work and false trails, the dead body of the child was found —but the kidnappers were never traced. A wave of threatened abductions subsequently swept the United States.

When Marlene returned home on the evening of Friday the 13th and proceeded to open her mail, she was confronted with an anonymous letter. The message was made up of printed letters taken from newspapers, strung together to form a threat to kidnap Maria unless she was prepared to pay a large sum of money for 'protection'. It also contained a long harangue against Marlene, and a threat of reprisals against Maria if the money were not paid.

Private detectives were at once engaged, several of them dressed as gardeners and servants. One of them was H M Reynolds, an experienced 'private eye' who later described this episode in Marlene's life:

'I was detailed, with a colleague, to direct the protection of the child. Some of the efforts made by gangsters to snatch little Maria now read like the purest thriller fiction. But I can vouch for the truth of them. The trouble started when she received the letter stating that unless she deposited fifty thousand dollars (about seventeen thousand pounds at today's rate of exchange) on a wall at the corner of Western and Sunset Boulevard, her daughter would be kidnapped and held for ransom.

'Miss Dietrich was frantic. She was almost unable to work. I set out to devise some scheme to give protection for the child, and at the same time trace the would-be kidnappers.'

The first move in the scheme was to prepare a package of imitation dollar notes, with an authentic dollar bill on top. Dietrich placed the package on the wall as the letter had demanded. Meanwhile Reynolds and another detective hid themselves and waited. In due course two men jumped from a taxi, snatched the packet from its hiding place and raced away again.

'They were too quick for us,' Reynolds said. 'The next day, Miss Dietrich received another letter demanding one hundred thousand dollars. This letter, assembled from newspaper cuttings like the first, said: "You, Marlene Dietrich, if you want to save Maria to be a screen star, pay. If you don't, she'll be a loving memory to you. Don't dare to call in detectives again." '

From that moment Marlene would never let Maria out of her sight. Reynolds accompanied her everywhere, eating at her table, scrutinising and passing her visitors, even standing guard at night in the room where she slept, with Maria in a cot by her side. Rudolph returned to share the vigils, and other friends, including Maurice Chevalier, offered their help. Shutters and bars were installed on all windows and approaches to the house, and the servants were armed.

'One day,' Reynolds remembers, 'we thought we would really test the kidnappers. We allowed little Maria to walk alone to the studios to meet her mother. Two detectives disguised to look like extras loafed along a few yards ahead, and my colleague and I followed at an equal distance behind.

'Presently we noticed a taxi crawling along beside Maria. There was nobody inside it—but we took the number, just in case.'

When they reached the studio entrance, the only person in

sight was an old lady in a long black dress and old-fashioned bonnet. She offered Maria a stick of candy. Then she looked up and became aware of four men approaching her. She ran with surprising agility towards the taxi-cab which was waiting just outside, and as she climbed in displayed an unmistakable length of trouser-leg.

The taxi-cab was traced, but the driver swore he knew nothing about his passenger and had dropped her somewhere in the centre of Los Angeles.

In all, some thirty people were held and questioned in connection with the attempted abduction of Maria Sieber, but the instigator was never traced.

CHAPTER FIFTEEN

Sternberg Must Direct

The kidnapping scare died away, but for some time Marlene kept doors and windows barred and bolted. The Department of Immigration, for some mysterious reason, advised her to send her German maids back to Berlin—it did not approve of aliens remaining in the household. Dietrich replied with typical loyalty and common sense. She pointed out that she had recently been employing eleven Americans, nine of whom were made necessary by the dangers of American life. The Department did not pursue the matter further.

Marlene was now living in the Bel Air mansion formerly owned by Colleen Moore. She gave few parties, none of them on the usual Hollywood scale, and still confined herself to a small group of friends. One in whose company she was often seen at this time was Maurice Chevalier, who had helped to watch the house at night during the threatened kidnapping. They had originally met at the Paramount studios, working on adjacent stages.

'At first we were merely fellow workers in the same studio,' Chevalier has said, 'but afterwards we became good friends. I used to go to her house and she would cook wonderful German dishes for me. Marlene really can cook. And she was always helping people—money did not count with her, it has never counted with her. She has great strength of character . . .'

An interview that Marlene gave to a journalist at this period bears out Chevalier's remarks. When he asked her whether it was fame and money that first attracted her to Hollywood, she replied quickly: 'No, I came to work with Mr von Sternberg. And I am not proud of being a film star—I have no reason to be. Compared with important professions, what I am doing is so unimportant.'

What, then, the reporter asked, did she consider her greatest accomplishments to date?

'I have a child,' Marlene answered. 'And,' she added, 'I have made a few people happy. That is all . . .'

The friendship between Marlene and Maurice Chevalier did not escape the attention of gossip columns. Rudolph, in Europe, would often arrange for Marlene's tailored suits to be made in Paris, and Chevalier, who usually returned to France in between films, would bring the suits back to Hollywood in his luggage. This arrangement was a favourite subject with columnists, who were as unable to understand the friendship between Chevalier, Dietrich and her husband as the one between Dietrich, her husband and von Sternberg.

With Rudolph for the moment in Europe and Marlene occasionally seen with Chevalier at restaurants and night clubs, the usual inferences were drawn. 'Few stars have been more outrageously maligned by the gossips,' Jules Furthman, who worked on the scripts of several of Marlene's pictures, has commented. 'Yet in three years I never heard her say a malicious word about any other person. In that respect alone she must be unique among feminine stars. She has borne it all as an inevitable accompaniment to movie fame.'

When von Sternberg returned from Europe, he had decided to abandon the circus story and set to work on the script of *The Scarlet Empress*, a life of Catherine the Great based on her private diaries. Meanwhile, the Paramount executives believed that a change of director for Marlene Dietrich would be in everybody's interests, and suggested to her that she might like to make *Song for Songs* for Rouben Mamoulian. Von Sternberg advised her to accept. He felt it would be good for her to experience a change of director.

Mamoulian, born in Russia, was a gifted and artistic director, a man of taste and imagination, who had worked on Broadway, producing the original version of *Porgy and Bess,* before coming to Hollywood in 1928, where he had made the first *Doctor Jekyll and Mr Hyde,* with Frederic March, and a highly successful musical, *Love Me Tonight,* with Jeannette Macdonald and Maurice Chevalier. Marlene had already heard about him, and their collaboration proved to be smooth and friendly. For her leading man, Brian Aherne was finally lured from the New York stage, where he had achieved a considerable reputation and had consistently refused all offers from Hollywood.

One scene in the script of *Song of Songs* called for a nude statue of the character played by Dietrich. An Italian sculptor called Scarpitta, who had won some renown by carving a statue of Mussolini on a horse, was employed to carry this out. When the film was shown, hundreds of enquiries were received in Paramount offices in various parts of the world as to whether Marlene had actually posed for the statue. Although Dietrich had paid several visits to the sculptor's studio, the official answer was, tactfully, that the work of art was the result of 'inspiration'. In a later scene in the film, Marlene had to hack it to pieces in a rage.

During shooting one day, Brian Aherne was standing near the statue, awaiting his cue for 'action'. At that moment, everything in the place reverberated—a slight earthquake tremor had passed through the city. Aherne noticed the statue swaying on its pedestal, and ran forward to catch it. But he was too late, and it fell. As it fell, he threw out his arms to clasp it, and held it against his body in a mock-heroic stance. A studio wit found the opportunity too good to overlook.

'You've saved the wrong Dietrich!' he shouted.

Song of Songs was a more successful film than *Blonde Venus.*

Paramount approached Marlene with a new contract which, if she had signed it, would have placed her among the three or four highest paid players in the world. The only people in Hollywood who had earned as much as Marlene was then offered were Tom Mix the cowboy star (who made more pictures per year than Marlene, of course), Marion Davies, then receiving a steady £2,000 a week, John Gilbert, and, for a year or two, Al Jolson.

Marlene, however, decided not to commit herself. She only agreed that her next film would be *The Scarlet Empress*, provided that von Sternberg directed it. And those who claimed that a rift was impending when Dietrich went to work for Mamoulian were wrong.

Actress and director probably devoted more care to *The Scarlet Empress* than to any of their previous films. The part of Sophia Frederica—the innocent girl taken from Germany to Russia to marry the insane Grand Duke Peter, and who gradually becomes involved in the intrigues of a decadent court, plots the overthrow of her husband, seizes his throne, and as Catherine the Great uses her sexual power over men as her chief political weapon— was dramatically more demanding than Marlene's previous roles. Her daughter Maria, incidentally, played Sophia as a little girl in the brief opening sequences. The settings were elaborate and costly. The Swiss sculptor Ballbusch and the German painter Kollorsz were brought in to work on the huge Byzantine decors. The Peterhof Palace with its grotesque sculptures and statuary was re-created in immense and impressive detail. Costumes were equally lavish, and one of Dietrich's superb court gowns was insured for three thousand pounds.

'I intend it to be not necessarily an authentic work, but something beautiful to appeal to the eye and the senses,' von Sternberg announced. Certainly no effort was spared; but the film was a resounding failure. It not only failed to attract significant numbers of the public—a serious blow for Paramount with a film as expensive as this—but received harsh critical notices. 'From picture to picture,' one critic wrote, 'von Sternberg has been slowly and surely devitalising Dietrich. Now comes the grand climax of that process in *The Scarlet Empress*. The film is a dreadful hodgepodge of sets. Full of gargoyles, confused episodes and action so vague and fleeting (as if von Sternberg were afraid of action) that you hardly know what is happening. Through this maze walks the beautiful, exciting Dietrich—a woman who could be such a splendid actress if properly guided, but who is slowly being spoiled because she believes every word that von Sternberg tells her about pictures, because she leaves her strong personal opinions at home . . .'

Paramount, not surprisingly, was uneasy. In those days, however, a director could survive commercial failure and differences of opinion with his producers far more easily than he can now. Today, from a Hollywood point of view, the story of the von Sternberg-Dietrich films seems curious enough—a major studio continuing to allow one of its most important stars to be handled almost exclusively by a director of increasing aestheticism and diminishing commercial success. *Blonde Venus* did reasonably well at the box-office, though disappointingly as a Dietrich film. *The Scarlet Empress* was almost disastrous. Nor could Paramount enjoy the consolation of approval from the critics. Though the visual beauty and technical skill of these films were rightly praised, they were almost universally condemned for their lack of real dramatic interest. Yet von Sternberg and Dietrich continued to work together as they wanted, with very little interference from their employers.

Shortly after *The Scarlet Empress* was released, B P Schulberg left Paramount and moved to Columbia. There were rumours that his departure had much to do with the dissatisfaction of shareholders in New York at his tolerant treatment of von Sternberg, his indulgence to his whims and demands. In fact, in spite of their many arguments, in spite of the episode over *Blonde Venus* that resulted in Marlene's suspension, the two men remained friends. Schulberg, for all his financial responsibilities, believed in von Sternberg's talent and was willing to take risks with it.

He was succeeded by Ernst Lubitsch, already famous for his witty and sophisticated comedies with music; he had been directing films in Berlin at the time of Dietrich's struggle to make a name for herself on the stage. The arrival of Lubitsch did not coincide with any change in Paramount's policy. He not only agreed to let von Sternberg make another film with Dietrich—the last he was due to direct for the studio under his present contract —but also persuaded Dietrich to sign a new longer-term contract. Under this she agreed to appear in two pictures a year at a salary of fifty thousand pounds a film.

The story of von Sternberg's next film was from a novel by Pierre Louys, *La Femme et le Pantin* (*The Woman and the Puppet*), previously made in 1920 with Geraldine Farrar as the ruthless Spanish seductress Conchita Perez. Lubitsch changed the title to *The Devil is a Woman*, and it went into production early in 1935—ironically enough just at the same time as Elisabeth Bergner, Dietrich's idol of the Berlin days, finished in England a version of *Catherine the Great* that was destined to become a great box-office success.

Marlene's new leading man was Joel McCrea, but within a week he had walked out of the picture, declaring he found it impossible to work under von Sternberg. 'All the spontaneity,' he complained, 'was being directed out of me.' Unperturbed, von Sternberg replaced him with a little-known young actor called Cesar Romero. In this film, too, he decided to take some of the credit previously awarded to his cameramen. He announced that it would be 'directed by Josef von Sternberg and photographed by Josef von Sternberg, assisted by Lucien Ballard'. For his last two or three films, von Sternberg as director had received little critical praise, but the camerawork in them all was greatly admired; and it is certainly true that von Sternberg knew as much about photography, knew how to obtain the effects he wanted, as Hollywood's leading cameramen. No matter with whom he has worked, the visual style of his films has been unmistakable.

During shooting, von Sternberg also stated that *The Devil is a Woman* would be his last picture with Dietrich. 'Fräulein Dietrich and I have progressed as far as possible together. My being with Dietrich any further will not help her or me. If we continued we would get into a pattern which would be harmful to both of us.' Dietrich only read about this in the papers, and for two days would not speak to her director. After this, however, their collaboration apparently progressed as before.

The result was a film with all the hallmarks of its predecessors. Von Sternberg's reconstruction of Seville at the turn of the century was richly exotic, packed with detail and expressive lighting effects. And Dietrich herself looked more beautiful than ever before. Many of her costumes had a frankly erotic quality, and their vivid Spanish style suited her wonderfully. Today *The Devil is a Woman* is still her favourite film. When asked why, she replies: 'Because I looked more lovely in that film than in any other of my whole career.' Von Sternberg has also pronounced it his personal favourite, although he has expressed himself as dissatisfied with all his work.

Dietrich again received what critical praise there was to secure, though in general the film was received as coldly as *The Scarlet Empress*. As well as this, the partnership of actress and director ended on a final note of misfortune. Six months after the film had been released, the Spanish Government formally protested to the American Government that it portrayed the Spanish Civil Guard in an unfavourable light. On the 31st October 1935, the Spanish Minister of War, Gil Robles, announced that every Paramount film would be banned in Spain unless *The Devil is a Woman* was immediately withdrawn from circulation all over the world. The State Department interceded, and agreement was finally reached that after fulfilling existing contracts for the film, Paramount would withdraw it. The Spanish demands were certainly unreasonable, as the film was not even set in the present day, but it was rumoured that the American Government was interested in concluding a trade treaty at the time.

At all events, the negative of *The Devil is a Woman* was destroyed, and only a few private prints of the film remain. And Miss Dietrich has one of them.

CHAPTER SIXTEEN

An Offer from Korda

Von Sternberg's Dietrich had officially ceased to exist, and the Marlene next to be seen in the cinema, in a story found for her by Lubitsch and produced by him, was a more human creature. Most important of all, perhaps, Lubitsch decided to bring the *femme fatale* up to date. For even when, in von Sternberg's films, the action was technically taking place in the present day, it was really in a never-never land. The court of Catherine the Great and the streets of Seville in the 1890s were hardly further away than what was supposed to be contemporary Vienna or Peking or New York. In his obsession with Marlene's extraordinary aloof glamour, von Sternberg isolated her completely. In her presence, nothing else had a real life of its own. Rooms, places and other people existed only to decorate Marlene, like the costumes she wore. These films were acts of homage, by a man of unusual taste, to the supreme physical beauty that Marlene embodied. He had placed her on a series of exquisite pedestals, and now she had to step down.

The beauty and the mysterious, languid personality that accompanied it had captured public imagination; but there was no doubt that the public wanted her to do more in her films than appear in a series of superb costumes and settings. It was Lubitsch's task to bring the legend, so to speak, down to earth. The story he chose was a romantic comedy called *Desire*, which cast Marlene as an international jewel thief finally reformed by the man with whom she falls in love. Her leading man was Gary

Cooper, with whom she had played in *Morocco*, and her director was Frank Borzage, noted for his popular and intimate romantic touch in films like *Seventh Heaven* and A *Farewell to Arms*.

'The new Dietrich' was a success. The public liked *Desire*, which skilfully preserved Marlene as a legend, but showed that the legend had a sense of humour. The *femme fatale* had become, in every sense, a woman of the world, and the secret behind the elegant, enigmatic face was simply that she lived by stealing necklaces in the best circles. It was a good joke and Marlene, not least of all, seemed to enjoy it.

Von Sternberg, meanwhile, rejoined Schulberg at Columbia, where he made a version of *Crime and Punishment* with Peter Lorre as Raskolnikov. When the film was released, critics were quick to point out that Marian Marsh, who played Sonya, was handled in a manner very similar to Dietrich.

Marlene at this time was seen a good deal in the company of a new friend, John Gilbert. Gilbert was then at the height of his popularity, receiving a fan mail of about sixteen thousand letters a week. He had been married three times, and was then married to Virginia Bruce, which failed to prevent long-standing rumours that he had been in love with Greta Garbo for years.

Dietrich's next film was negotiated for her by Lubitsch, who loaned her to David Selznick's company for *The Garden of Allah*. This, her first film in Technicolor, was the somewhat improbable story of a world-weary American heiress who has a brief romantic encounter with a monk who has renounced his vows on the edge of the desert. It later transpired that Selznick had originally committed himself to giving Merle Oberon the leading role, for as soon as shooting started she served a writ on him for damages of twenty-five thousand pounds. Her claim seems to have been strong, for Selznick shortly announced that 'an amicable settlement out of court has been made in the case brought by the

British actress.' The settlement cost him eighteen thousand pounds.

To play the monk, Selznick engaged Charles Boyer, whose presence and voice in his first American film quickly won him popularity. Within a year he was starring with Garbo. It was, indeed, the appeal of its two stars that ensured a moderate success for *The Garden of Allah*, a film at times verging on the ludicrous and, in its weird Moroccan atmosphere and desert settings, suggesting a parody of von Sternberg.

The Arizona desert actually served for the Sahara in this film, and Dietrich recalls the oppressive heat and frequent sandstorms. 'The heat made some of the company ill,' she recalls, 'and once it got me, too. You may remember a scene where Basil Rathbone, jumping from his horse, greets me outside his tent. In that scene I fainted, and did not come round for several minutes. I suppose it was sunstroke.'

This was the second time that Dietrich had fainted, the first being on location for *Morocco*. Just as she was coming round, she realised that a member of the unit was about to throw water in her face. 'Is there to be another close-up?' she asked von Sternberg at once, for although only just coming out of her faint she remembered that water would spoil her make-up. 'The word is close-up, not *cloze-up*,' von Sternberg replied.

After *The Garden of Allah*, Dietrich received an offer from Alexander Korda to make a film in England. Ironically enough, von Sternberg had just been obliged to abandon a film he had started for Korda. This was a version of Robert Graves' *I, Claudius*; after a few weeks' shooting, the unlucky Merle Oberon was injured in a car accident, and to have restarted production with a different star would have caused difficulties with the contracts of other leading players. The film that Korda proposed to Dietrich was an adaptation of James Hilton's *Knight Without*

Armour, with Robert Donat as her leading man and Jacques Feyder as director.

Dietrich accepted, and signed a contract which gave her fifty thousand pounds for her part in the film. A surprise awaited her, however, as she prepared to leave for England. United States income tax officials presented her with a formidable demand for tax claims, and refused her permission to leave the country until at least a part of them were satisfied. Finally, they accepted emeralds and other jewellery worth twenty-eight thousand pounds, and allowed her to embark on the *Normandie*.

For some time before this incident Dietrich had been battling with the tax authorities, and about five years after this incident she was to be victorious. Perhaps the Treasury Department should have heeded the shrewd critic who wrote of Marlene that she gave him the feeling she would always be 'two steps ahead in making a bargain.' For Marlene and her husband were finally victorious to the tune of ninety-five thousand dollars. The Treasury Department not only dropped their claims but admitted that the actress had overpaid a substantial sum.

CHAPTER SEVENTEEN

Filming in England

The Marlene who arrived in England for *Knight Without Armour* in May 1936 was more like the Marlene of *Desire* than of the von Sternberg pictures. Besieged on her arrival by reporters and columnists, she answered their questions with good humour and a shade of irony. To the newspaper man who asked her whether she liked travelling, she said that she enjoyed a change of scene. Invited to state her views on men, she pronounced: 'I would rather be a man because men have clearer and better brains. There is no advantage in being a woman.'

The main topic of conversation at that time was Edward VIII's romance with Mrs Wallis Simpson, and the likelihood of his abdication. The night before the news finally broke, Dietrich was rehearsing a sketch with Douglas Fairbanks Jnr on the stage of the Coliseum Theatre for an all-American variety performance in aid of charity. Edward G Robinson, another performer in the show, came in with a newspaper bearing the headline, *The King May Abdicate Today*. This was enough to interrupt the rehearsal, and the entire cast began discussing the news. Dietrich read the story and then turned to Fairbanks.

'Doug,' she said, 'call up the King and say we are coming down to Fort Belvedere. You've got his telephone number, haven't you?'

Fairbanks and the rest of the cast were, not unnaturally, taken aback. 'But we can't do that,' he said at last.

Marlene was adamant. She really seemed to believe that she could persuade King Edward to change his mind. She was certainly determined to try, for the next day she travelled down to Fort Belvedere. However, she was stopped at the entrance and informed that an interview could not be granted.

In London, Marlene met many friends—Douglas Fairbanks Jnr, Noël Coward, Cecil Beaton. She was often seen in the company of Fairbanks, particularly at first nights and premières. One evening she arrived at the Leicester Square Theatre for a première. As she passed through the crowd into the brilliantly lit foyer, a voice called out, 'Two to one Mae West!' There was a similar incident at another première, when the Master of Ceremonies introduced her to the audience. 'We have with us tonight the great artist of the screen—Miss Marlene Dietrich,' he proclaimed; and a loud Cockney retort was heard from the gallery: 'So what?'

These were rude solitary voices. For Dietrich was a success in London, both with the crowds who mobbed her and with the 'Four Hundred'. And she easily out-dazzled British stars at public appearances. At Denham Studios, too, she quickly won the affection of technicians, who admired her good humour and her sound craftsmanship. She often made quiet, shrewd suggestions about lighting or wardrobe problems or camera set-ups; and her working knowledge of film-making was by now remarkable. Dietrich recalls that the technicians offered to pay her a penny for every original suggestion she gave them. 'Do you know,' she comments, 'that shooting wasn't far advanced before I'd clocked up three-and-sixpence?'

'The new Dietrich' was broadening her sense of humour. Just as, not long before, Korda had met her at a Hollywood party, her arm round the neck of her friend Fritz Lang, chewing happily on the same stick of celery with him, so now she munched sticky chocolate bars on the set at Denham and had to wipe her sticky fingers wherever she could. Also, Korda had received a whimsical cable from Wally Westmore, the Hollywood make-up expert, shortly after Dietrich's arrival. It had been a curious fact that, for all their erotic atmosphere and themes, her films with von Stern-berg contained hardly any direct love-scenes. But now things had changed. 'For Heaven's sake watch her make-up,' Westmore cabled. 'She needs a new mouth after every kiss. This Dietrich has become the hardest kisser in movies.'

The script of *Knight Without Armour* called for a bathroom scene, and when the shot came to be filmed all studio workers not directly concerned with it were ordered off the set. A 'prop' man stood by, ready to churn the bath water into a bubbling white foam. When he actually did so, he spilt a little by accident on to the fake marble floor. Dietrich, with the assistance of a wardrobe girl, took off her wrap and stepped into the bath. When the shot was filmed, she reached to lift herself out, covered herself in the wrap, and stepped cautiously to the floor. Suddenly she lost control of her wrap, and slipped to the floor, her famous legs pointing up wildly into the air. But she was quite unhurt, and drily amused. 'Thank God,' she remarked, picking herself up, 'there's no continuity to *that* shot!'

During the making of *Knight Without Armour*, Dietrich received some disturbing news of her friends in Hitler's Germany and Austria. It is said that her willing intervention in many cases cost her a fortune. If it did, Marlene herself has never spoken of the money she spent in this cause. At all events, several of her old friends, threatened with Nazi persecution, in effect came to owe her their lives, for she provided air tickets and financial guaran-tees that brought them to safety in England or America.

The visitor who came to see Marlene in her dressing-room at Denham one day knew nothing of this. Rudolph, who had come over from Berlin, was there, and also the German-born journalist and writer, Willi Frischauer. Word was brought that a blonde actress called Mady Soyka, whom Marlene had met in Berlin,

85

wanted to see her urgently. Marlene seemed amused by the news.

'It might be extremely interesting,' she said, and Frischauer recalls that it was. Mady Soyka had come to London on behalf of Dr Josef Goebbels, with an offer which they both hoped would attract Marlene back to Berlin and increase the artistic prestige of Nazi Germany. The offer was fifty thousand pounds in any currency, tax-free, for one film, with complete freedom to choose her story, leading man and director, and an option for three more pictures on the same terms. Marlene replied with a decisive refusal.

Mady Soyka returned to Berlin. She became an important figure in the Nazi entertainment world, and was in Paris during the German occupation. Shortly before the end of the war she was killed by members of the French Resistance.

During week-ends, and when she was not required on the set for a few days, Marlene used to visit Paris, principally to see Erich Maria Remarque, author of *All Quiet on the Western Front*, who had become a close friend. In London she enjoyed fashionable night-life, mainly in the company of Fairbanks, occasionally with Cecil Beaton. Beaton took some exquisite photographs of her, but shortly afterwards published some not particularly amicable impressions of her in *Cecil Beaton's Scrapbook*.

'The most striking of her features,' he wrote, 'is her whiteness, which would put the moon or a white rabbit to shame, even though, as she explains, she uses a powder darker than the colour of her skin. Instead of eyebrows, she has limned butterflies' antennae on her forehead . . . Her figure is heavier than one had imagined, her head heroically carried on hunched shoulders and, to make her hands appear more slender, she grows her finger nails quite two inches long . . .

'But to describe her in detail is beside the point, for she now *feels* sufficiently beautiful to convince other people, with her panoply of affected surprise and wonder, of moistened lips, tentative shoulder shrugs, and dewy eyes, framed in a setting of mushroom colour with slightly puffy underlids that make her look as if she were about to abandon herself to a sneeze . . .

'Once, in Salzburg, I went to see her in her hotel, and took a camera with me. She had a cold in the head and no make-up on, but she whipped out of bed and posed in every conceivable position, for two dozen photographic time-exposures, concluding with a pleading attitude on the floor with her head against the tablecloth, starry-eyed, lips apart, yearning towards the empty tea-cups and the remains of the marzipan cakes above her.

'Dietrich will break any number of appointments without a tremor, and while those at the cocktail party given in her honour are speculating as to what has become of her, she will be sitting in an ordinary, impersonal hotel room, wearing a dressing-gown, or the exaggerated mannikin suit of the ventriloquist's doll, a half-empty box of gold-tipped cigarettes on a side table, a bowl of fruit and tomatoes on the sideboard, plucking her eyebrows, stroking her arms, vaguely waiting for a long-distance telephone call . . .'

Beaton concluded, after an incisive dismissal of most of her films, by hoping that Dietrich would turn back from the exaggerated glamour of Hollywood and do more that was worthy of her 'beauty and sensibility'.

This article was later reprinted in a popular daily newspaper under the title, 'Hollywood Stars Debunked.'

Before she left England, Marlene, at her own request, visited the Hospital for Sick Children in Great Ormond Street. 'If I could have chosen my profession I would have been a nurse,' she informed the matron. 'I think it must be wonderful to feel that you're doing so much good for people.'

In a black costume, embroidered with gold, she entered a ward full of excited children, all with autograph books at the ready. A tiny little Welsh girl, Myfanwy Evans, staggered forward to present a bunch of red roses almost twice as big as herself. The occasion proved too much for her, and she began to cry.

'Oh, darling!' Marlene exclaimed, and snatching the little girl in her arms began quickly and effectively to console her. 'I have learnt such a lot this afternoon,' Marlene said later. 'My little daughter Maria wants to be a doctor, and is also very interested in nursing. I wanted to find out all about it to tell her.'

CHAPTER EIGHTEEN

No Return to Germany

When Dietrich returned to Hollywood after making *Knight Without Armour,* she decided to become an American citizen. Coming shortly after her dismissal of Mady Soyka, this action no doubt angered the Nazi Government, for she was violently attacked by Julius Streicher, editor of the anti-Jewish newspaper *Der Stuermer.* 'The German-born Marlene Dietrich has spent so many years among the film Jews of Hollywood,' he wrote, 'that she now becomes an American citizen. Frequent contact with Jews renders her entirely un-German.' The article was accompanied by a photograph showing Dietrich at the oath-taking ceremony.

Marlene received the attack without surprise, commenting mildly that of course there were Jews in Hollywood, of course she mixed with them, and they happened to make good pictures. She was far more concerned with her reunion with Maria, now almost twelve, who was overjoyed to see her. And she has never returned to play in Germany.

There was also a new film waiting to be made. Lubitsch had prepared a story for her which he was going to produce and direct himself. It was a high society comedy called *Angel,* and Dietrich was to play a beautiful woman mistaken for a Grand Duchess and pursued by a young American adventurer. She had two leading men this time, Melvyn Douglas and Herbert Marshall. *Angel* was a light, sophisticated film in the Lubitsch manner, and enjoyed more success than *Knight Without Armour,* a slow and fairly improbable spy story.

In spite of this, Dietrich and Paramount came to the parting of the ways after *Angel*. She had been under contract to the studio for seven years, and had become one of its biggest and most widely publicised stars. But the announcement from Paramount ending the association was almost pointedly brief. 'Marlene Dietrich,' it said, 'will be permitted to work elsewhere.' Star and studio, it appeared, had disagreed irrevocably over the terms of a new contract.

Marlene seemed to enjoy her new freedom, and was in no hurry to make another film. Beginning with *The Blue Angel*, she had starred in twelve films in nine years. Now, for the next eighteen months, she travelled a good deal—to New York, London, Paris, the French Riviera. She was seen at the casinos in Monte Carlo and Cannes, she was seen on the beach and at restaurants with Noël Coward, Alfred Lunt and Lynn Fontanne, and she went to dinner with Somerset Maugham at his villa at Cap Ferrat. Her social life during this period was, in fact, what is usually described as 'exclusive'.

For one of her visits to London, she rented a flat in Grosvenor Square, and one evening received a personal call from the former German Ambassador to the Court of St James', Joachim von Ribbentrop. After a great many compliments, it emerged that the point of his call was, once more, to tempt her back to Berlin. In addition to the most generous contracts and conditions, Marlene was also promised this time a triumphal entry into the German capital with Hitler himself to greet her.

When Marlene said she was not interested, the diplomat begged her at least to have dinner with him and continue the discussion. But this, too, she refused.

As well as her extremely active social life at this time, which took her into the houses of politicians and aristocrats as well as artists, Marlene became increasingly occupied with another pursuit. It had begun, perhaps, on that evening in the twenties when her

Berlin landlady had told what the cards predicted for a struggling and melancholic young actress. At any rate, she had come firmly to believe in the power of astrological prediction. She was convinced, and still is today, that the stars in their courses may be consulted for guidance about the future. For many years now she has mapped her own life by the stars, with the aid of Carroll Richter, a New York astrologer in whom she has great confidence.

Was it, then, at the direction of her Capricornian balance that she returned to Hollywood in 1939 to attempt something which presented her with a challenge and promised an entirely new lease of screen life? For it was the offer of a highly unconventional role in a film called *Destry Rides Again* which brought her back to America.

Joseph Pasternak, another Berliner whose career had begun at the end of the first World War, was at this time a leading Hollywood producer, with a number of musicals and the discovery of Deanna Durbin to his credit. He now planned a picture that was to satirise the Hollywood Western, and he wanted Dietrich to play the leading role of a tough, hot-tempered bar-room entertainer called Frenchy.

When a star is uncertain what to do next, the advice most frequently received is: 'Change your type, dear.' It was advice that Marlene decided to heed, and her performance as the saloon queen in *Destry Rides Again* turned out a success on every level. She sang a number that became a popular hit—*See What the Boys in the Back Room Will Have*—and she performed with a humour and verve that proved decisively she had a range beyond romantic confections and boudoir comedy.

She was also, in this film, to take part in what was alliteratively described by the studio's publicity department as 'The Greatest Feminine Fist Fight Ever Filmed'. The sequence involved several minutes of hair-tearing and face-scratching action between Una Merkel and Marlene, which ended with the former losing her skirt and the latter being soaked with a bucket of water. When the film had been released and was a success, Marlene commented: 'To think that after all these years it was a brawl and not a love scene that took me right to the top and kept me there.'

Destry Rides Again was released a few weeks after the outbreak of World War Two. In its early stages the conflict made no direct impact upon the lives of average American citizens, and certainly not of Marlene Dietrich, except that she worried about friends in the danger zones of Europe. Pasternak, meanwhile, was asked by his studio, Universal International, to find another subject for Dietrich, and came up with a story called *Seven Sinners* which offered her a part somewhat reminiscent of Sadie Thompson. This time she played Bijou, a sultry, trouble-making South Seas café singer who falls in love with an American naval officer. Her leading man was John Wayne, in whose company Marlene was often seen outside the studios during the making of the film.

Also during the shooting of *Seven Sinners*, Marlene was informed by her astrologer Carroll Richter that Paris would fall that year to the Germans. She thought at once of her friends in France, particularly of Erich Maria Remarque, and begged him by cable to leave Paris as soon as possible. A few days before the German Army entered, he did so.

Another refugee from France at the same time was the brilliant director René Clair, whom Pasternak chose to make Marlene's next film, *The Flame of New Orleans*. This was a light romantic comedy, set in New Orleans during the 1840s, about an adventuress who poses as an aristocrat and has most of the town at her feet. Like *Seven Sinners* it had a considerable success, and as a result of her films for Universal International Dietrich remained a star with a wide public.

Shortly after *The Flame of New Orleans* was finished, Richter telephoned to warn her that at all costs she must not report for work at the studios next day, where she was due to make a test. She decided, uncharacteristically, to disobey the warning, and was walking across the set when she tripped over a coil of arc-lamp cables, and broke her leg. When she telephoned Richter to confess the result of her disobedience, he told her not to worry—the leg would heal more quickly than she expected.

When the leg was set in plaster, Marlene sent a message to Herbert Marshall, with whom she had appeared in *Angel*. Marshall had lost a leg in the first World War, and later embarked on a Hollywood career with a false leg, concealing it so effectively that it was imperceptible on the screen except to people who already knew. Marshall gave Marlene a course on how to walk without disclosing a limp, and within a fortnight of the accident she was back on the set with scarcely a sign of one. When the plaster was removed, the leg was found to have suffered no imperfections whatsoever.

CHAPTER NINETEEN

The Reverse of Retirement

In 1941 American newspapers were full of reports that Dietrich intended to retire. The cause of them was an interview she had given to a reporter in which she remarked: 'Of course I'm going to quit working. I want a chance really to see a bit of life before I die.' She explained that she had reached the point when she was tired of entertaining people, and wanted to settle down to a quiet home life with her husband and daughter. 'A film star's career must necessarily be brief,' she added. 'It can last only as long as one's youth lasts, and one's youth fades far quicker on the screen than on the stage. The public can be fooled on the stage, but never on the screen—and I'm going to quit while I'm still at the top.' Only one person in the world, she considered, would be able to maintain her glamour for life. That was Garbo 'She has a magic quality which will survive bad pictures—and even age . . .'

But Dietrich was not yet thirty-eight, and her glamour was obviously unimpaired. She seemed, in fact, to forget her intention to retire very quickly, for she was soon filming again—at Warners this time, in a triangle drama called *Manpower*, with Edward G Robinson and George Raft, and she followed this at once with a comedy, *The Lady is Willing*, in which she played an eccentric Broadway star who kidnapped a child.

She was, as it happened, at a difficult stage in her relationship with her own daughter at this time. Maria, now sixteen, had probably been slowly developing the usual complexes about being a daughter of a beautiful and famous star. Today she is a beautiful woman in her own right, but throughout her early childhood Maria was something of a plain girl, inclined to plumpness. Her mother had tried to disguise this in the way she dressed her, but the child was always aware of her shortcomings and was troubled by them. She was lonely and withdrawn. Since the attempted kidnapping she had been sent to boarding school in Switzerland for six months of each year, and she later recalled that 'the guards who were hired to keep a day and night watch on me became my only friends. They used to send me letters and jars of peanut butter . . .'

When Maria was five years old she had become known as the 'First Hollywood Baby', because of her frequent visits to the set when her mother was filming. Studio executives had wanted to keep the child as much in the background as possible in case her existence should detract from Marlene's aura of glamour. They considered the public should not know that Marlene had a growing child—it wasn't good for the glamour business. But Marlene took a different view, insisting that her daughter visit her at work, introducing her to the technicians. Reporters and photographers became interested, and Dietrich discovered that, inadvertently, she had started a fashion. As pictures appeared in magazines, other stars began to follow suit, and before long it had become fashionable for Hollywood mothers to admit to their children in public.

But for Maria the publicity was discomforting. 'Mother was so beautiful,' she explains, 'that her beauty always gave me a feeling of ugliness and unworthiness. I felt my mother should be ashamed of me.'

At school in Switzerland, her sense of solitude and frustration increased, and she grew correspondingly plumper. Food, in fact, became a consolation. She devoured quantities of cakes and sweet things. 'The fatter I got, the more I suffered. And the more I suffered, the more I ate. Naturally, since I was Marlene Dietrich's daughter, people expected me to be beautiful. But I wasn't beautiful. Even later on when I tried to lose weight I couldn't. Diets had no effect on me, I just continued to put on pounds.'

She became obsessed with her mother's beauty. 'I remember how I used to cry at night. I remember a whiff of perfume and my mother in furs standing there in my room, looking so beautiful. I was so jealous when she went out—I knew that she was dressing up for someone else, and that she wanted to see someone else rather than me.' Another time she saw her in the kitchen at home, wearing the white maid's uniform that she assumed for cooking, unmade-up and her hair in pin-curls, and 'she was so beautiful she took my breath away'.

Meanwhile, Marlene went on to two more films. She returned to Universal for *The Spoilers*, directed by the veteran Frank Lloyd who had made *Cavalcade* and *Mutiny on the Bounty*, and in which she played Cherry Malotte, owner of an Alaskan gin palace, and was reunited with John Wayne. She starred with Wayne again in *Pittsburg*, which consolidated her success as a saloon heroine.

But with these two films, another cycle in her career ended. Since leaving Paramount in 1937, Dietrich's work had been somewhat uneven. Although most of her films had been successful enough, and she had retained a strong following, their level had noticeably changed. Apart from René Clair, she had not been directed by an outstanding personality, but by various efficient Hollywood craftsmen, experienced entertainment purveyors. Although *Destry Rides Again* was original and revealed a new side to her personality, her only subsequent film of real distinction had been the one with Clair, *The Flame of New Orleans*. Most of the others offered her less good variations on the *Destry* role, and were of no more than average quality. Dietrich was, once again, in danger of being trapped in a formula.

Perhaps she herself was aware of this. At any rate, *Pittsburg*

With Maria

Above: In 1934

Below: Circa 1950

Above: With Jean Gabin and Raimu
Below: With Jean Gabin

With Basil Rathbone at a Hollywood party

Above: 'You may now smoke.' Savoy Hotel, London 1951, with toastmaster John Mills
Below: Cooking in a Paris restaurant

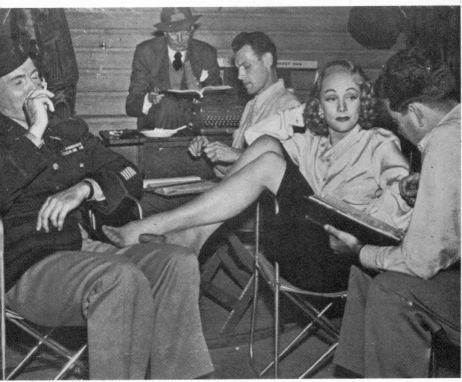

Above: With Alfred Hitchcock on the set of *Stage Fright*
Below: Making *A Foreign Affair*

Above: With Noël Coward (and Douglas Fairbanks, Jnr, centre right)
Below: With René Clair making *The Flame of New Orleans*

1954—liberation of Paris ceremony

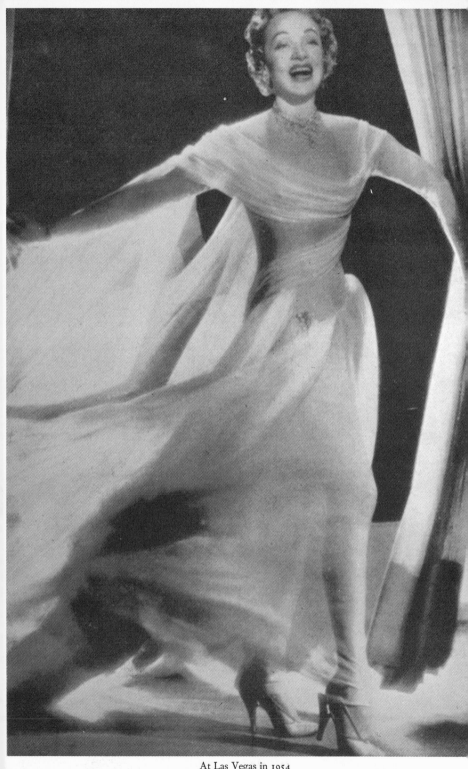

At Las Vegas in 1954

Café
de Paris,
London
1954

An autograph, England 1951

One of Dietrich's oldest friends, Noël Coward, greets the star on her arrival in London for a cabaret season (1954)

Dietrich takes a shy at a coconut at a Garden Party in aid of blind children (July, 1954)

With the late Charles Laughton and (*left*) Director Billy Wilder and Producer Arthur Hornblower Jnr on the set of *Witness for the Prosecution* (1957)

With Orson Welles during a break from shooting *Touch of Evil* (1958)

With Spencer Tracy in *Judgment at Nuremberg* (1961)

Arriving at a full cinema for a performance of *Black Fox*, Dietrich seats herself on the floor of the stalls next to property millionaire Felix Fenston and his wife, formerly Greta Borg. In the film Dietrich narrates the story of the rise of Hitler

With the Beatles while rehearsing for the British Royal Variety Performance (November, 1963)

Below: With Her Majesty The Queen Mother at a Royal Film Performance in London

Below: Producer Robert Nesbitt lines up his star cast, headed by Marlene Dietrich, for the finale of a Royal Variety Performance in London. *Left to right:* Wilfred Brambell, Harry H Corbett, Beatles George Harrison and John Lennon, Buddy Greco, Harry Secombe, Tommy Steele, Dietrich, Charlie Drake, Nadia Nerina, and Flanders and Swann

October 1966. Marlene, escorted by three police officers, is mobbed by enthusiastic fans as she leaves the stage door of the Golders Green Hippodrome. This was the first night of her British tour which was a tremendous success. Her daughter, Maria, attended her every performance closed the bar-room period, and her next appearance was something of a surprise. Universal were preparing a revue-style film specially slanted for members of the United States forces, and recruiting a variety of talent that included W C Fields, George Raft, Vera Zorina and Dinah Shore. Another star of *Follow the Boys* was to be Orson Welles, who had decided to do a magician act—magic being one of his favourite hobbies. A lovely lady was required to be put in a box and sawn in half by Welles for this act. Dietrich accepted this brief but picturesque assignment, which proved to be one of the most popular sketches in the film.

She followed this with a rather undistinguished film, *Kismet*, from Edward Knoblock's oriental romance, in which she appeared as a queen of old Baghdad. Its chief interest was an exotic dance for which the famous legs were encased in shimmering gold paint. By the time shooting ended, Marlene had decided that the next thing she did would be very different.

CHAPTER TWENTY

Close to the Front Line

Early in March 1943, Marlene Dietrich contacted the United States Entertainment Organisation (USO), equivalent to Britain's wartime ENSA, and arranged to do an extensive tour of liberated countries, to entertain not only serving troops but also the liberated peoples. She landed in North Africa a few weeks later, and gave her first performance to members of the Allied armies at the Algiers Opera House.

The show began with a comedian coming on the stage and announcing that Miss Dietrich would be unable to appear as she had gone out to dinner with an American colonel. As groans of disappointment began, a voice called out from the back of the auditorium, 'No, I'm here!' and a moment later the slim, immaculate, khaki-clad figure of Dietrich ran down the centre aisle carrying a strange, tapering leather case.

Friends had noticed that for many years Dietrich carried this case as part of her luggage, and wondered what was inside. Now Dietrich made her revelation. After apologising for her lateness, she sat down, opened her bag, produced a pair of evening shoes and put them on. Then she produced an evening frock, took off her khaki tunic and was apparently about to change her skirt on stage when she was discreetly led to the wings, to the obvious disappointment of applauding troops. In a moment she returned in evening dress, and after a comedy act with other members of the show, launched into *See What the Boys in the Back Room Will Have*. Other favourites followed, and then she opened the strangely shaped leather case.

Inside was an ordinary carpenter's saw and a violin bow. Marlene sat down, put the wooden handle of the saw between her exquisite knees, and played a tune on it.

'I bought the saw in Austria in 1927,' she said afterwards. 'I learnt to play it for my own amusement, and then—well, I thought I'd bring it to my show to amuse the soldiers. I had a try-out in the States to see how the boys liked it.'

Then she went home to her villa, and experienced her first air-raid. The sirens sounded and the lights went out as she opened her front door, and she went out to her balcony to watch the anti-aircraft shells exploding over the sea, and saw a German plane shot down.

A few days later she conducted a Press conference, at the special request of war correspondents. She entered the War Conference Room of the military headquarters at Algiers in her elegant khaki uniform, sat down and crossed her khaki-covered legs while a string of questions was put to her. One correspondent remarked afterwards that she looked barely thirty, and all commented on the head-dress she had designed to wear with her peaked Army cap. It resembled a fine crêpe khaki bandage, which she swathed round her head and allowed to fall loosely over one shoulder. She told the correspondents that she expected to remain in the North African theatre of operations for about three months, that she wanted to give open-air shows, and that she hoped to visit England before returning to Hollywood. She also revealed that she had brought four dozen pairs of silk stockings with her.

Not long afterwards Marlene went out to a French warship to give a show, and was presented with a bouquet of red and white carnations from the crew. Her next stop was Anzio, where she lived in conditions primitive enough to give the lie to allegations of celebrities being accorded privileged treatment. Like the troops themselves she washed her face in the snow, ate out of mess-tins and once helped some American soldiers to shift an overturned jeep from a quagmire. (Subsequent reports that she lived in a rat-infested dug-out were exaggerated.) And in the evenings she put on her evening dress and silk stockings and sang *Annie Doesn't Live Here Any More, Miss Otis Regrets, Taking a Chance on Love, There I Go Again,* and many others to large and appreciative audiences.

In September 1944 she came to London, and was visited by a photographer at the Savoy Hotel, whose request for a leg picture she refused, as she was in uniform. She looked up many old friends, and appeared rather briefly at the Stage Door Canteen—only long enough, according to one disgruntled newspaper report, to say, 'Good evening, fellows, it's swell seeing you!' After the liberation of Paris, she flew over and sang to Allied officers at the Bal Tabarin. She also saw Jean Gabin again, whom she had first met during his exile in Hollywood.

Now under the control of SHAEF, she started off on another series of tours, entertaining hundreds of thousands of troops and civilians on a variety of improvised stages. She performed in North Africa, Sicily, Italy, England, France, Belgium, Czechoslovakia, Labrador, Greenland and Iceland. When she arrived at Prestwick Airport from Iceland, she was to experience an odd situation. Having been invited by the military authorities to make a tour of the defence area by motor coach, she was taken aback, on getting into the coach, to see that a dozen bemedalled German generals were her fellow passengers. Each of them sat rigid, looking straight ahead, apparently oblivious of the only woman in the coach. The military policeman escorting Marlene nodded in the direction of the generals and suggested that she tell them who she was. The generals, suddenly aware of her presence, stepped smartly to attention and saluted in characteristic Prussian fashion.

For once in her life Marlene was completely nonplussed. She simply did not know what to do. She murmured a nervous 'How do you do?', looked at the rows of medals, and fled. It is the only time on record that she has lost her poise in public.

About this time it was rumoured that Dietrich's long-standing interest in astrology had broadened to include telepathy. Was it true, somebody asked her, that she had been practising telepathy when serving in the forward battle areas? She only smiled. 'Overseas,' she told her questioner, 'it is never hard to read a soldier's mind.'

The wits who had suggested that Marlene Dietrich had been sent to the war to 'lift morale by lifting her skirts' were firmly discountenanced by her enthusiastic and workmanlike approach to the task. She flew in unpressurised military aircraft at eighteen thousand feet, travelled by jeep, lorry, landing craft and almost every type of service vehicle. She even drew praise from the formidable General Patton, whose unpublished diaries are said to contain several approving references to her. In between spells of duty, on a visit home, she was approached by the Office of Political Warfare to record a number of her hit songs. These were translated into German and given a propagandist twist. The idea seemed strongly to appeal to her, and afterwards she remarked: 'I've often been dissatisfied with my work. But by recording these "adapted" songs I believe I have done something really worthwhile.'

It was by now a legend that wherever Marlene appeared in the war areas, every soldier she met wanted to kiss her. She rationed kisses to those about to take part in imminent battle, recalling later: 'The war gave me the opportunity of kissing more soldiers than any other woman in the world.' She was also frequently asked about her gold-painted legs in *Kismet*, advance news of which had reached the troops, who were impatient to see the result.

In March 1945 Marlene appeared at the newly created Stage

Door Canteen in Paris—not in uniform this time, but in an off-white muslin blouse and black skirt. She came on to the stage backed by an orchestra and was greeted with a flourish of trumpets from the *Garde Republicaine* in full dress. It was a star-studded occasion that also included Noël Coward and Maurice Chevalier.

A few months later there occurred a much grimmer event. After Mady Soyka's visit to her on the set of *Knight Without Armour*, Marlene had announced vehemently that she would never return to Germany. But now she decided to go to Berlin to see her mother, and also to find news of her sister Elisabeth, rumoured to have been sent to a concentration camp.

She found Frau von Losch, whom she had not seen for more than six years; but it was believed that Elisabeth might be in Belsen, which had just been liberated. Marlene went there to search for her and, to her intense joy and relief, discovered she was one of the survivors of that terrible camp. She took her back to Berlin, and it must have been a strange, rather desolate family reunion in that ruined city.

Returning to Los Angeles in 1947, Marlene was decorated with the Medal of Freedom, the highest decoration the American War Department can give to a civilian. The citation reads:

'Miss Marlene Dietrich, civilian volunteer with the United States Service Organisation Camp Shows, performed meritorious service in support of military operations in North Africa, Sicily and Italy from April 14 to June 16, 1944, and in the North Atlantic Bases in Europe from August 30, 1944 to July 13, 1945, meeting a gruelling schedule of performances under battle conditions, during adverse weather and despite risk to her life. Although her health was failing, Miss Dietrich continued to bring pleasure and cheer to more than five hundred thousand American soldiers. With commendable energy and sincerity she contributed immeasurably to the welfare of the troops in these theatres.'

The reference to Marlene's health was not exaggerated. For some time before the end of her tour she had been far from well, having suffered a bout of pneumonia which penicillin cleared up, and going straight into hospital for a jaw operation on her return to America.

She subsequently went back to Europe for a third tour, playing in Germany, in various hospitals, and lecturing on films at the Army University in Biarritz. She fell victim to a severe attack of influenza, and after her recovery ended her Army career by playing for four weeks at the Olympia Theatre in Paris.

General Omar Bradley was to add his tribute. 'Many of us came to admire Marlene's spirit and to appreciate her contribution because she was so much interested in entertaining our soldiers over a long period of time, and because she quite often visited very close to the front lines.' But the final tribute was to come from France. At a private ceremony in New York, French Ambassador Henri Bonnet presented Marlene Dietrich with the medal of the *Lègion d'Honneur*.

CHAPTER TWENTY-ONE

Maria Marries

With peace declared, Marlene wanted to return to films. The war had considerably depleted her financial resources, and it had become important for her to work again. She and Jean Gabin were approached by the French director Marcel Carné, whose previous film had been the enormously successful *Les Enfants du Paradis*, to star together in his next production, a study of life in post-war Paris to be called *Les Portes de la Nuit*. Marlene liked the idea of making a film in Europe, and of playing with Gabin, who had become a close friend. They had met first in Hollywood—Gabin escaped from France in 1940—then in wartime Algiers, and again in Paris after the Liberation.

Negotiations proceeded over the film, but finally both Dietrich and Gabin decided that the parts were not suitable for them. (*Les Portes de la Nuit* was subsequently made with an unknown actress, Nathalie Nattier, in Dietrich's part, and introduced Yves Montand to the screen in the role originally offered to Gabin. It was a costly and serious failure.) However, they found another subject that they liked better, *Martin Roumagnac*, a triangle drama set in a French provincial town, with Marlene as a beautiful widow and Gabin as a builder, her social inferior, in love with her. Another member of the cast was Margo Lion, the cabaret artist with whom Marlene had appeared on the Berlin stage in *Something in the Air*.

Martin Roumagnac was Marlene's first film in Europe since *The Blue Angel*, and the first she had ever made in French.

During its making she was constantly seen in Gabin's company, and the usual rumours followed them. But a few days after shooting finished she left France, and some weeks later Gabin married a young French actress.

The film itself was generally held to be disappointing. More might have been expected from such an interesting pair of leading players.

The life of Marlene Dietrich's daughter Maria, meanwhile, had not been smooth. She had passed through an unsettled adolescence, still suffering from a childlike, possessive jealousy of her mother, still disturbed by her plumpness. As she grew older, she withdrew into books. She read avidly, and as a result developed a sudden interest in medicine. She studied innumerable books on disease, surgery and psychoanalysis, and thought about becoming a doctor. Then she decided on something very different.

Maria knew that almost every studio in Hollywood would be interested in her as Marlene Dietrich's daughter, and she now made up her mind to go on the stage. Not because she really wanted to, but to prove something to herself. Max Reinhardt, who had taught her mother so much, had emigrated to America in the thirties and for several years had been running an Academy of Acting in Hollywood. Maria joined his Academy, not from love of the theatre, but, as she said, 'as a form of shock therapy. Knowing full well what would be the effect on the audience of discovering that the big heavy girl on the stage was the daughter of Marlene Dietrich. Also, because the thing held a certain challenge for me. I was curious to find out whether a person like myself, who weighed a full one hundred and eighty pounds at the time, could successfully portray roles that are commonly associated with irresistible women.'

Maria went out of her way to avoid trading on her mother's name, and after acting in many of Reinhardt's Academy productions, set out as Maria Palmer to try the New York stage. She managed to gain a small role in the Theatre Guild production of *Foolish Notion*, starring Tallulah Bankhead.

Shortly before leaving Hollywood, she had made a brief, disastrous marriage to a drama critic named Dean Goodman. She was eighteen at the time, and it was mainly the failure of the marriage that decided her to go to New York. She did not enjoy her part in *Foolish Notion*, however, and considered she was not suitable for comedy. She managed to gain her release from the cast, and joined a USO company in the wake of her mother, who was then in Europe with the American forces. In June 1946 she returned to New York, twenty-two years old and still sadly overweight. She learned that a job was open at Fordham University for an actress to give a graduate course in acting and direction; she applied for it and was given the post. This was to prove a turning point in her life.

One afternoon in that late October Maria was taking a rehearsal of her campus production of *Peer Gynt*. Examining the stage, she decided that a blue spotlight was marring the effect of a scene, and called out for it to be removed. A voice in reply suggested that she might care to mind her own business.

The voice belonged to a man whom Maria described as 'tall, dark, hungry-looking', and who moved 'with the grace of a leopard'. He looked about twenty-five, and was probably of Italian origin. It was love at first sight, and she married William Riva, a stage designer, in the following July. They had very little money, but would not accept help from Marlene, in the usual independent way of young married couples. They did, however, accept a refrigerator from her. The young couple set up home in a somewhat ramshackle apartment house, and for a year or so struggled to make ends meet like many other young couples.

Marlene, meanwhile, received an offer to return to Paramount, a studio for which she had not worked since they disagreed over contractual terms in 1937. Mitchell Leisen, who had previously directed her in *The Lady is Willing,* wanted her to star in *Golden Earrings,* the story of a gipsy used as a secret agent by British Intelligence during the war. The film was highly implausible and not particularly well received, but it provided Marlene—in dark hair, a swarthy make-up, a variety of gipsy scarves and costumes and, of course, golden earrings—with an exotic and unexpected part for her return to Hollywood. And her next role, her most successful for some time, was to re-establish her firmly.

This was in *A Foreign Affair,* a cynical comedy set in post-war Berlin. The director, Billy Wilder, had been a crime reporter in the German capital during the twenties, while Marlene was a film extra. He came to Hollywood in the thirties, and in collaboration with Charles Brackett wrote some successful comedies for Lubitsch (*Bluebeard's Eighth Wife, Ninotchka*) before becoming a leading director with *Double Indemnity.* Wilder now had the shrewd idea of re-creating Dietrich in another kind of Lola-Lola role, as a night-club singer in the Berlin of 1947.

A Foreign Affair was a film she particularly enjoyed making, and once more the husky, sinuous voice had some suitably world-weary numbers to sing—including *Black Market* and *In the Ruins of Berlin*—composed by Friedrich Hollander, who had written her songs for *The Blue Angel.* When shooting was finished, the Johnston Office ordered retakes on one night-club scene in which, it alleged, the Dietrich legs were over-exposed.

Some time later, walking with a friend down Times Square, Dietrich noticed the statue of a naked woman that peers hugely down from the roof of a famous clothing store. 'I often wonder about this American morality,' she remarked. 'That statue hasn't even got panties on, but if I so much as show the tops of my stockings, they slap me down . . .'

CHAPTER TWENTY-TWO

Glamorous Grandmother

When Maria gave birth to a son in the middle of 1948, it seemed that the usual mother and daughter problems had been solved. Maria decided to abandon her acting career and devote herself to being a full-time wife and mother, and Marlene was delighted by her daughter's obvious happiness. The news of John Michael's birth spread round the world, and it was not long before Marlene was dubbed 'The World's Most Glamorous Grandmother', a title which no journalist has apparently ever allowed himself to forget.

Some time later Ed Sullivan, ebullient host of the American *Toast of the Town* television programme, introduced 'Grandma Dietrich' to a vast audience at Madison Square Garden. 'I got more whistles from the audience than I ever had,' the grandmother calmly recalls.

Marlene now spent much time at her daughter's home. She enjoyed helping with household chores, tidying the child's nursery. No doubt she re-lived some of the experiences when Maria herself was born. There is a story that she used to help with the child's laundry, and that she was once stopped by a taxi-driver in the street at three o'clock in the morning with a bundle of washing under her arm. 'He took me for a Third Avenue washerwoman, and was most sympathetic about the long hours I worked. I hadn't the heart to explain to him that I was then living at the Plaza Hotel, so I got him to drop me several blocks away in a poor quarter, and walked back to the Plaza when he was out of sight.'

In May 1950 a second child, John Peter, was born to Maria and William. Maria emerged from this phase a supremely happy young woman, and—as if shedding all her previous unhappiness—she underwent a physical transformation. She started losing weight. Without any effort by way of dieting, she continued to shed pounds—sixty-five in all. When she consulted doctors, they explained that a metabolic change had caused her weight to adjust itself. Marlene's daughter now felt that she might start again as an actress and telephoned an agent she knew. When he saw her, he was enthusiastic, and within two weeks she made her television début.

It was not, however, a glamorous part. Maria played a dowdy, down-at-heel Viennese chambermaid—but her notices were excellent, and she had two offers from Hollywood as a result. Maria, though, did not want to go to Hollywood. William had by now a good deal of work as a designer in New York, and she was determined to maintain her home. She persevered in television, and soon the Rivas moved to a charming four-storeyed house in the fashionable East 90s.

Maria had now achieved what her mother had long enjoyed—a star dressing-room, with 'Maria Riva' on the door.

In the summer of 1950 Alfred Hitchcock sent Marlene the script of his forthcoming thriller, *Stage Fright*, to be made in England. He wanted her to play the part of Charlotte, a famous musical comedy star. Marlene accepted, met Hitchcock in New York, and arranged to start filming at Elstree in the autumn.

Dietrich did not go straight to England for the film, but flew first to Paris for consultations and fittings at the Christian Dior salon. The script of *Stage Fright* specified a number of glamorous costumes, and Dietrich insisted that Dior create her wardrobe. It cost something like £2,000.

Hitchcock, meanwhile, announced an impressive cast for his

picture—Michael Wilding, Jane Wyman, Richard Todd and Alastair Sim as well as Marlene. In England, everyone was waiting for Marlene to arrive. A dressing-room at Elstree studios was re-decorated, a suite was booked at Claridges. Ben Lyon, then producing his *Hi! Gang* radio programme, tried to contact her in Paris to invite her to take part in the show, but was informed that Marlene was 'not available'. The star did, however, contact Elstree studios with suggestions for publicising her wardrobe.

Finally she arrived at London Airport at midnight, and walked into the lounge in a smart French costume and a wide-brimmed hat. She looked tired and unsmiling. A photographer asked her to sit down on a stool, which she obligingly did. But when he asked her for a leg picture, she gave him a rather ambiguous smile.

'If it's true that my legs are my fortune,' she said, 'why should I show them to you for nothing?'

There was a brief, uncertain silence. Dietrich pulled up her skirt no more than half an inch, waited while the cameras clicked, then walked out to her car.

Next day she was guest of honour at a Press luncheon at the Savoy. More than three hundred Pressmen, representing newspapers, magazines, radio and TV programmes, had been invited. Dietrich, dressed completely in black and looking slim and elegant, talked with Press representatives in the River Room until the red-coated toastmaster called the guests to lunch.

Marlene sat in the centre at a long table, next to Richard Todd and Robert Clark, production chief of the Elstree studios. Throughout the meal she was observed to chain-smoke, and ate little food. When coffee was served, the toastmaster rapped the table with his gavel.

'My Lords, Ladies and Gentlemen,' he called, 'the toast is— His Majesty the King.'

Everyone stood up, raised their glasses and drank. Dietrich sat down again, puffing at her cigarette.

The toastmaster again rapped the table. 'Ladies and Gentlemen—you may now smoke.'

There was a sudden silence, as everyone looked at Dietrich, at that moment withdrawing her cigarette holder from her mouth. Then people began to laugh. Dietrich appeared nonplussed—she looked first at her cigarette, then at the toastmaster, and then she blushed—one of the first blushes she has ever displayed. Used to smoking between courses, she had forgotten this British formality of not smoking before the Royal Toast . . .

The photographers immediately became busy, but Marlene retained her composure. She smiled, whispered an apology to the toastmaster, and conversation sprang up again. Then she rose and walked calmly out of the room.

CHAPTER TWENTY-THREE

England and Hitchcock

Immediately after Dietrich left the Press luncheon and retired downstairs, two members of the editorial staff of *Picture Post*, Lionel Birch and Harry Deverson, asked the Elstree publicity director if she would be able to spare them five minutes for a talk. Although the *Picture Post* photographer had taken dozens of Dietrich pictures for a feature in the magazine, Birch and Deverson felt the star might be able to help them extend the story.

Dietrich received them in a private suite below the River Room, and conversation began.

DEVERSON: 'Miss Dietrich—we are thrilled with the pictures we've got, but we feel there might be some idea, something you might suggest perhaps . . . that might heighten the effectiveness of our photo feature on you . . .'

DIETRICH: 'Such as . . . ?'

DEVERSON: 'Frankly, we're not quite sure. We felt we might take more pictures of you—at the races, perhaps, or a society ball . . .'

DIETRICH (*puffing at cigarette*): 'Go on . . .'

BIRCH: 'Well—er—Miss Dietrich, let me put it like this. We might suggest your being photographed in Bond Street—or some other fashionable place—or . . .'

DIETRICH: 'Yes, you might suggest that.'

BIRCH (*now clutching at almost any straw*): 'Look, Miss Dietrich. Isn't there *anything* you have *not* been photographed doing?'

A pause. Dietrich looks at Birch, gives a half-smile, puffs on her cigarette.

DIETRICH: 'Yes.'

The feature appeared as originally planned, with no additional photographs.

Marlene had been contracted for *Stage Fright* at a salary generally described as 'fabulous'. It was said at the studios that a Dietrich contract was something well worth studying, a tribute to a star with an unusually astute and uncompromising business sense. If you wanted Dietrich for a film, you were virtually bound to sign a contract on her terms, considered to constitute the most efficient and thorough legal document ever seen in the film business. Otherwise, you didn't get her.

When she arrived at Elstree studios to make her first lighting test, it was late afternoon, and most of the people concerned were placed on overtime. Hitchcock was waiting for the star on Stage One, surrounded by technicians, make-up men, wardrobe assistants and hairdressers. The camera crew had trained the camera on a small chair and table, raised on a rostrum.

Wearing a smart Parisian costume, Marlene was formally introduced by Hitchcock to the technicians. Now, most of the staff at Associated British are accustomed to passing international stars in the corridors, with hardly a second glance. But on this occasion all the other studio workers who should have been on their way home were discreetly watching—from the edge of the set, in doorways, beside stage flats.

Wilkie Cooper, director of photography on *Stage Fright*, asked Dietrich to take up her position on the chair. She sat down, crossed her legs, then looked round the set, took stock of the lighting gantry. After a moment she pointed out to Cooper exactly the lights that he should use in making the test, and where they should be placed.

Cooper was polite but clearly disconcerted. He had already heard that Dietrich made a habit of telling cameramen exactly how to photograph her. But afterwards, when asked how, as an experienced lighting director, he reacted to Dietrich's instructions, he replied: 'Well, you know, I had heard tales of Dietrich and her lighting tricks, and I must be honest and say I didn't take too kindly to her telling me how to do my job. After all, I had lit many famous stars and many famous pictures. However, I thought I'd let her have her own way, and when it was found to be wrong, I would then do it my way. I'm bound to tell you in honesty that she was right about her lighting. Dead right. For the close-up stuff, I couldn't have improved upon it.'

A clause in Dietrich's contract stipulated that no still photographs of herself should be issued by the studio to the Press until she personally had passed the proofs. When she posed for portraits, the prints were first sent to her, and she would send them back to the photographer with a detailed letter of instruction about whatever retouching she considered necessary. Frank Buckingham, the studio's still photographer, considered her the most 'patient and co-operative' star with whom he had ever worked. 'At the end of a whole day's still photographic session,' he recalled, 'she was always eager to continue being photographed.'

Hitchcock himself, with a note of dryness, paid tribute to Marlene's extensive knowledge and experience. 'Marlene Dietrich is a professional,' he remarked. 'A professional actress, a professional cameraman, a professional dress designer . . .'

It was during the shooting of *Stage Fright* that Marlene began another close friendship, with Michael Wilding. They were frequently seen together, on and off the set. They were fond of driving, and used to go out to Great Fosters, Egham, for cocktails; they dined at the Caprice, where the restaurateur received Marlene as if she were royalty, and sometimes sent round food by car if she dined at a friend's flat. Marlene also visited Noël Coward and went to one or two of Cecil Beaton's parties.

One new acquaintance sounded a discordant note. This was Anton Walbrook, to whom she was introduced one evening at

Mischa Spoliansky's flat. Afterwards he said: 'I did not know Dietrich in Berlin or Vienna. I had heard much about her—her intellect, her glamour, her wit and her charm.'

Spoliansky, whom of course Marlene had known since the twenties in Berlin, had renounced Germany when the Nazis came to power and taken out British citizenship papers. He had achieved considerable success as a composer for films and the theatre in Britain and America. Spoliansky and his wife Eddy were among the small circle of Marlene's really close friends in London, and their Hampstead flat was often a kind of retreat for the star. When she wanted to relax completely, Marlene would be driven out there, and for an evening she could speak her native German and help cook the dinner. Sometimes she took Michael Wilding with her.

It was at one of her evenings with the Spolianskys that she made a remark which led to the achievement of a long-standing ambition.

When Marlene Dietrich, Michael Wilding and Eddy and Mischa Spoliansky were gathered round the sitting-room fire after an informal meal cooked by Eddy and Mischa, conversation turned to the nature of fame. Marlene looked serious. 'Although I've been lucky in meeting famous people in many walks of life—letters, politics, business, the theatre and films,' she said, 'with some exceptions, Michael, they bore me. I would much rather meet scientists—they give so much to humanity. I sometimes wish that I had been a scientist—someone like Sir Alexander Fleming. He's done so much for mankind, I think I admire him more than any other single person. I wish so much,' she repeated, 'that I could meet him.'

Eddy Spoliansky said that she thought she could arrange it, as she knew one of Sir Alexander's greatest friends; and a few days later she succeeded. Professor Hindle, the bacteriologist, telephoned to say that Sir Alexander would like to meet Miss Dietrich. 'Fix it up and he'll come.'

For the next few days Dietrich spoke of little else. She ordered an exquisite blue silk dress for the occasion; she telephoned to Erich Maria Remarque, her close friend in Paris, to get his suggestions for wine, and she telephoned Eddy Spoliansky regularly to discuss details of the arrangements. Finally, when she prepared to leave Elstree for Hampstead on the evening of the party, Joan Smallwood, her hairdresser at the studio, remembers Marlene being 'as excited as a schoolgirl'.

There were six at dinner: Sir Alexander Fleming, Professor Edward Hindle, Marlene, Michael Wilding, and the Spolianskys. It was a gay, happy occasion. Dietrich had persuaded Eddy Spoliansky to telephone Professor Hindle to discover Sir Alexander's favourite food. Unknown to either Eddy or Marlene, the Professor had in turn telephoned Sir Alexander—and in fact what they ate had been suggested by Fleming himself, and only he and the Professor knew it. When this came out in conversation, it added to the high spirits of the party.

Dietrich talked long and enthusiastically to Sir Alexander about her wartime experiences, about penicillin and the war-wounded. She mentioned that she had often seen for herself the efficiency of Sir Alexander's discovery, and also how she had heard of many instances of penicillin curing venereal disease.

At this, Sir Alexander smiled in his enigmatic, benign manner and looked over his glasses. 'That,' he said, 'is one of the diseases penicillin cannot cure, Miss Dietrich.'

Later she asked him if he would autograph his photograph, which Spoliansky had thoughtfully provided. He laughed and said that although he had never signed a picture of himself in his life for anyone, he would make an exception. Then he produced from his pocket a small glass jar containing a culture of penicillin, and handed it to Marlene with the signed photograph. She was delighted. She snatched at the container and everyone laughed at her eagerness.

This meeting with Sir Alexander Fleming began a friendship that was kept up by correspondence and occasional meetings to the time of his death in March 1955. He liked Marlene for herself, not as a film star, for, as he admitted: 'I haven't seen any of her films. I don't know what people mean by glamour, but I recognise in Miss Dietrich an intelligent and brilliantly witty person.'

CHAPTER TWENTY-FOUR

Royal Performance

During the autumn of 1950, when *Stage Fright* had already been shooting for several weeks, Marlene Dietrich was invited to appear at the Royal Film Performance, in the presence of his late Majesty King George VI, Queen Elizabeth and other members of the Royal Family. As usual, the film itself was to be followed by an elaborate stage production, involving the services of many visiting stars from the United States as well as British actors and actresses. The late Nat Karson, at that time producer of the stage show, accepted Ben Lyon's offer of collaboration, and the two of them set about working out different kinds of personal appearances for the stars.

They were not sure at first how Dietrich could best be included, until Ben Lyon suddenly conceived a number that he thought would be ideal for her. Dietrich was at this time spending a few days in Paris, since Hitchcock was filming scenes in which she did not appear, and Lyon—who had known her in the early Hollywood days—telephoned the star at the Georges V Hotel. He explained his scheme, which involved a specially written song and dance act. Since Marlene had recently achieved wide publicity by becoming a grandmother, he felt this might be used to good advantage and he visualised her doing a satirical song called *We're All in Love with Grandmother*—in company with, he hoped, Michael Wilding, John Mills, himself, Jack Hawkins and, perhaps, John Gielgud.

Lyon sketched the idea to Marlene on the phone with his customary enthusiasm, and ended by asking her what she thought.

There was a short pause before Marlene, who had said\ ably little during the conversation, answered. 'How dare y\ said, and rang off, probably because she felt the proposal was out of keeping with the dignity of a royal occasion.

When Marlene returned from Paris it was decided that she would be given a solo spot in the Royal Show and sing her celebrated *Lili Marlene*, which she had performed with great success during her wartime tours. Somebody suggested giving her a painted desert backdrop for the number, but she declined the offer, preferring to appear simply in front of the curtains.

On the Sunday morning before the day of the show, she arrived at the cinema to rehearse the finale, for which the entire cast of stars was to be presented *en bloc* to the Royal Party. All the female stars were wearing dresses which they had had specially designed for the occasion, but few were not discomposed by Marlene's appearance—for she entered the theatre in a mink *dress*, a costume made up entirely of mink skins.

The night itself passed off with customary glitter: thousands of fans outside the cinema in Leicester Square, pressing against the police barrier and screaming with delight whenever a favourite arrived, flashlights, exquisite gowns and white ties and tails in the foyer. Marlene came on towards the end of the show, stepped into the glare of a single spotlight, and began the famous number:

> *Underneath the lamplight,*
> *By the barrack gate,*
> *Darling, I remember,*
> *The way you used to wait . . .*

The trace of Berlinese in the husky, assured voice remained. At the end of the song, the audience applauded—but not vociferously, for this was a British Royal occasion at which enthusiasm was tempered with dignity.

Dietrich walked off into the wings, where a crowd of stars was assembled. She looked downcast, believing that her song had not been well received. After being presented to the Royal Party, she took part in the finale number and was one of the first to leave the cinema—by a back door. Michael Wilding helped her into her waiting Rolls, which had the distinction of being the only star limousine granted a special escort of two policemen on motor cycles.

During *Stage Fright*, the studio employed as Dietrich's personal dresser a girl named Babs Gray, whose job it was to see to the star's wants in her dressing-room and on the set. Babs Gray had to care for the Dior wardrobe worn by Dietrich in the film, and knew that the star was particular about the care of her clothes. Immediately she discarded a dress for the day, Babs Gray had strict orders to iron it and to hang it carefully. The star is even meticulous about stockings, wearing a new pair of nylons every day.

'Some days,' her dresser remembers, 'she was sweet and reasonable—others she couldn't be bothered to talk to me.' Dietrich, who also used a new cigarette holder for each cigarette, would invariably smoke it down about halfway and then, if Babs happened to be in the room, pass it to her to finish.

Dietrich is a woman whose extreme individuality is reflected in her personal appearance. Her perfume, a Dior perfume, is exclusive to her, and her shoes, specially made in Paris, are always slipped on and off by means of two buttons. Ferragamo, the famous shoe-maker, remarked during her fittings for *Stage Fright* that 'Marlene Dietrich has the most beautiful feet in the world'. Her dresser, who confirms this, discovered that they were size two and a half. As soon as she entered her dressing-room to relax, however, the star invariably took off her beautiful shoes and issued the command: 'Pass me the old mules.' Babs Gray also remembers that Marlene had a passion for taking baths, and a habit of leaving jewellery and valuables anywhere. Several thousand pounds' worth of rubies or diamonds, of which she is particularly fond, would be left loose on her dressing-table or in the main wardrobe. Hours later she would ask casually: 'What did I do with my jewellery—have you seen the stuff?'

Marlene never attended the executive restaurant for meals while filming at Elstree. She would eat only biscuits, drink only tea, and take an occasional glass of champagne after finishing work for the day. 'You sensed when you were near her,' Babs Gray remarked, 'that she was a real star—much bigger, and more individual, than the average run of stars. Although she had an official make-up artist at her elbow for the picture, she always made herself up. With her own make-up, too, which she had brought from Hollywood.' The star had, indeed, once been presented with a union card by Hollywood make-up artists, bearing the citation: 'You know as much about this business as we do . . .'

Always considerate to her dresser, Marlene gave her a characteristic present at the end of shooting: a pair of black ear-rings, with necklace to match, which she had brought over from France. 'I spent each and every day with her,' Babs Gray has said. 'But I never got close to her. Few people do, you know . . .'

CHAPTER TWENTY-FIVE

No Highway

The first intimation to the British film world that Marlene Dietrich was returning to England in 1951 for another film was a cable received by Joan Smallwood, who had been the star's hairdresser on *Stage Fright*. It asked whether she would be free to work on Marlene's next film. Joan had first met Dietrich at Denham studios in 1936, during the production of *Knight Without Armour*, and her gay personality had endeared itself to the star. She cabled back in the affirmative.

Dietrich returned to London from Paris, was met at the airport by Rolls, and drove to Claridges, where Michael Wilding was waiting to greet her. At the hotel, she faced the British Press again.

'I am not ashamed of being forty-four,' she said. 'And I am proud to be a grandmother twice over.' This remark was no doubt a reference to the fact that, when she returned to America after making *Stage Fright*, the United States Federation of Grandmothers' Clubs—with a membership five million strong—had elected her 'America's Most Romantic Grandmother'. The title of 'The World's Most Glamorous Grandmother' had been won by a short head by Gloria Swanson.

Marlene's new film was *No Highway*, from Nevil Shute's novel, in which she played a glamorous film star, one of the passengers on an adventurous transatlantic air journey. It was to be shot at Denham, where she had first worked in England fifteen years previously, and the start of production was a happy event for everyone concerned—for these were depression days in British films, and the new film brought back to work two hundred and fifty studio technicians who had been dismissed ten months earlier when the studios closed down. Marlene's co-stars were James Stewart (with whom she had previously played in *Destry Rides Again*) as the eccentric 'boffin', and Glynis Johns as the air hostess; and her director was Henry Koster, yet another Berlin émigré who had frequented the Berlin theatrical cafés in the twenties. There was to be no Dior wardrobe this time, although, as Margaret Furse, dress designer for the film, said, Marlene's costumes would be 'very much the kind she wears in real life'.

When she arrived at Claridges, the star's real life costume was in fact a Dior creation, a black fur-trimmed suit with a wide swagger coat. On her lapel she wore the tiny red and yellow ribbon of the Medal of Freedom. She was also suffering from a heavy cold, and told reporters: 'I'm full of penicillin and drugs—I should be in bed.'

During her visit, reporters became very inquisitive over the question of Marlene's age. When she remarked, 'I wish people wouldn't give my age as forty-seven,' they asked for the correct figure and were told, 'I'm forty-four. I suppose people think I'm older because I'm a grandmother. But I was married when I was very young.' When an acquaintance commented, 'I've heard estimates ranging from forty-seven to fifty-seven,' Marlene replied, 'I've decided the best idea when people ask my age is to say I'm seventy-one and let it go at that. Someone told me the *Encyclopaedia of Names* has my right age—I don't know, I haven't seen it.'

One of Marlene's early scenes in *No Highway* took place inside an air-liner built on the Denham set. The film was for once to be shot largely in continuity, and Marlene expressed her dislike of filming last scenes first and vice versa. 'Thank goodness,' she said, 'I'm starting this picture at the beginning. I can't get used to the idea, despite my twenty odd years in films, of beginning a movie with the final scenes.' She was asked if she had any ambitions to fulfil. 'No,' she said, 'none at all—I've never had any secret desires. I just want to keep on making pictures because I'm in the groove.'

A few days later 20th Century Fox, producers of the film, gave a Press reception for Marlene at the Dorchester. One of those present was Walter Rilla, the German actor and playwright who, many years ago, had starred in a film in Berlin on which Marlene had had a few days' work. He had been invited by Henry Koster to meet Marlene again, and though they spoke little to each other after the introduction—'Marlene, you remember Walter Rilla?' 'Of course, how are you?'—Rilla remembered that, throughout the party, Marlene was casting discreet sidelong glances in his direction.

He wondered what was passing through her mind—memories of the old days, of her personal struggle when Rilla was a famous name in the German theatre and she was unknown? But he couldn't be sure, for she said nothing, and her expression was inscrutable.

On the set of *No Highway*, Marlene would drink hot coffee from a silver thermos jug, poured into a red and gold Rockingham cup. She went on location to the Royal Aircraft Establishment at Farnborough wearing a £3,000 mink coat. A little boy there was so eager to watch the filming that, in running forward, he tripped over, fell on the ground and burst into tears. Marlene heard his weeping, rushed over and knelt down to comfort him. It was this kind of gesture that won her the whole-hearted approval of the unit, for whom—since the weather was intensely cold during location shooting—she ordered rum at her own expense.

Yet, in spite of her popularity, Dietrich did not seem to be happy at Denham. Her mood was usually solitary and distant, she complained of the long walk from her car to the set, and there were stories of tension with another member of the cast—though she was kind and attentive to young Janette Scott, who played James Stewart's daughter in the film. She never ate in the studio restaurant, remaining in her dressing-room with Joan Smallwood, who worried that she ate so little. The first attempt at remedying this, however, did not turn out quite as expected.

While preparing her own lunch, Joan Smallwood pressed Marlene to join her in a snack. The star finally agreed, sat down—'she used to hate to sit down,' Joan remembers—and was passed a tray of cold meat and salad dressed with mayonnaise. Suddenly the tray slipped and its entire contents spread over the beautiful Balmain dress she was wearing. But Dietrich made no fuss. She quietly poured some warm water from the sink, knelt on the floor, and sponged the salad cream from her dress.

Marlene used to receive many telephone calls in her dressing-room. 'Famous people would ring up every day,' Joan Smallwood recalls. 'But if Marlene wasn't in the mood, she simply wouldn't talk to them—however famous they were.' She used also to carry round with her, as she still does, a small case containing a wide variety of pills, which she would administer freely to any friend suffering from an ailment. Despite differences of opinion occasionally on the set between the star and Glynis Johns, they were not evident when Glynis Johns, during one of the last days of shooting, complained of feeling ill. Dietrich immediately telephoned her own doctor and asked him to come round.

Joan Smallwood remembers how restless Marlene appeared during the making of No Highway. She seemed unable to sit still or to become passive in any way in front of other people; she was sometimes like a caged animal. She was almost certainly in a tense, nervous state at the time. One day she received a letter from her daughter Maria who, with her youngest son John Peter, had seen her off at La Guardia airfield. Maria mentioned in the letter how, after the plane had taken off, the roar of the engines had frightened the child, who finally burst into tears. As Marlene read this passage to a friend, tears came into her own eyes.

Marlene's love of children was more than once displayed during the making of *No Highway*. When Joan Smallwood's little daughter contracted an illness, Dietrich used anxiously to enquire about her progress each day. One morning she arrived in her dressing-room carrying a box, and asked Joan to turn her back while she opened it. 'You can turn round now,' she said a moment later, and held up a beautiful child's dress. She had taken the trouble to discover the child's exact measurements, and arranged for the dress to be made in France and flown over.

This was not the only example of her consideration for others, a quality that always survived personal changes of mood. Joan Smallwood's husband, Neville, a studio make-up artist, had served in the RAF during the war and been shot down off Dunkirk. During his term in a POW camp, he had arranged for his wireless operator to call on Joan in England with a present. This was a topaz ring, which naturally acquired great sentimental value for her. One day Joan came to the studios upset and preoccupied, and Marlene discovered that she had lost the ring. During the lunch period, unknown to Joan, the star sent her chauffeur to Bond Street to look for a ring with an identical setting. The chauffeur returned with several, and Dietrich laid them out on the dressing-table.

'I want you to choose the one nearest to the ring you lost,' she said.

At the end of the film she presented everyone of the set with a parcelled and labelled half-bottle of gin, each label written out in her own hand.

By the time Dietrich finished *No Highway* and returned to America, *Stage Fright* had been released. The reception was lukewarm;

critics considered it below Hitchcock's usual level, and Dietrich herself received little praise for her role. She hoped for better notices for *No Highway*, and was not to be disappointed. The film was generally liked, and most people judged Dietrich's performance as the best she had given for years.

Marlene spent the Christmas of 1951 with her family in New York. Maria and her two sons were waiting on the Manhattan quayside as the *Queen Elizabeth* docked, and Marlene's grandchildren were overjoyed to see 'Missy', as they called her, again. Maria and Bill had now firmly established themselves in American television, and Marlene proved herself to be her daughter's most active champion. When Maria prepared for a play, Marlene made a habit of sitting in the control booth, proudly watching and assessing her daughter's moves. 'Marlene has great love for her daughter—too much love, almost,' a well-known director commented at this time. Mercedes MacCambridge, the film and television actress, also remarked how 'all Marlene's friends get wires from her whenever Maria is on television. The wires give the time, the day and the network.'

CHAPTER TWENTY-SIX

Las Vegas

Marlene had not been back in the United States for long before RKO-Radio approached her with the offer of a new film. The part was on the lines of *Destry Rides Again,* but the project appealed to her because the director was to be the famous Fritz Lang, another link with the UFA days, whom she had often met at Hollywood parties and whose work she admired. *Rancho Notorious* turned out to be a western which, although it enjoyed a good commercial success, hardly advanced the reputation of star or director. But Marlene enjoyed making it, and won the admiration of her leading man, Mel Ferrer, who pronounced: 'The word for Marlene is Erda—the earth goddess.'

When the film was finished she went to New York, where she was often seen in the company of Erich Maria Remarque, Ernest Hemingway, and publisher Iva Patcevitch, senior executive of the Conde-Nast publishing company (*Vogue,* etc). She also started her own radio programme for the ABC network, a series called *Café Istanbul.* This was a dramatic series in which she had little opportunity to sing, although she occasionally interpolated a few bars of a favourite like *La Vie en Rose.* 'It's a hell of a job to do a dramatic show in half an hour,' she said. 'There just isn't time for singing because you have to worry about character and plot.' But she took the show as seriously as she takes everything in which she has a real interest, often staying up until the early hours of the morning, tapping out on a typewriter with one finger pages of revisions to the script. Once again her professionalism was acknowledged, and the producer of the show, Leonard Blair, publicly paid tribute to her. 'Marlene is a worker—a hard worker. She really rolls up her sleeves . . .'

Dietrich has always tried to avoid discussing her friends in public, and evaded the questions of over-inquisitive reporters. But one, during this time, was more persistent than the others. He wanted to know all about her friends—how long she had known them, whom she most liked, and so on. 'I just can't answer those questions,' Dietrich said, but her interviewer seemed undaunted. 'Who is the man,' he pursued, 'you most admire?'

For a moment Dietrich looked away from him, then she answered slowly and quietly: 'Mr Remarque . . . But I don't see him very often now.'

Close friends of both had known for a long time that Remarque greatly admired Marlene and her ability to help him overcome the spells of melancholia, to which he was addicted. His only recorded comment on Marlene is: 'She is a very great and generous artist, and a very great personality.' But Hollywood tells an eloquent anecdote about them: 'Dietrich and Remarque saw a great deal of each other for a number of years,' a friend once said. 'I was present, I believe, when it ended. She had given him an aquarium full of tropical fish—including three she especially admired. These she had called "The French Fleet", because they had the French tricolor on their tails. Remarque treasured the gift; he would clean the aquarium every day. Then after some time, it began to show signs of neglect. One night, at a dinner party at his place, Dietrich looked at the aquarium and saw some fish floating on the surface, dead—including "The French Fleet". The dinner went very badly. She kept referring to the fish, and everybody at the table could feel her disappointment. We left immediately . . . I don't think that was one of the happiest of dinner parties.'

There was a scene in *No Highway* in which Marlene Dietrich, playing the film star in the air-liner, is told that the tail of the plane is destined, according to mathematical calculation, to fall off at any moment. Thinking that she may be killed, the star muses a little on the achievements of her life, the meaning of her success. 'A few cans of celluloid on the junk-heap some day,' she murmurs.

One doesn't know whether the irony of the line occurred to her then, but it is certain that two years later, early in 1953, she decided to begin a new career for herself—as a cabaret entertainer.

In the post-war years, an enormous publicity campaign had informed the world of the emergence of a boom town in the Nevada desert; in its arid wastes a town called Las Vegas had slowly been expanding. Luxury hotels, gambling saloons and night clubs had been promoted by a group of businessmen who had combined with the Nevada authorities to provide 'French dressing in an early West background'. In an atmosphere of Bar X ranchers and cow-punchers, an embodiment of the screen's boom town had sprung into existence; and, at the same time, the desert had also become the testing ground of the United States Atomic Organisation. Not far from the casinos and the hotels, atomic bombs were exploded from time to time, and the luxury town's unflinching publicists were quick to exploit even this. 'There's always something going on in Las Vegas,' their advertising announced, with photographs of leading hotels set off in a central display of the crimson, yellow and grey of an atomic bomb in the process of exploding.

Many famous stars, from America and Europe, were offered fabulous sums to appear in cabaret at Las Vegas, and when the Hotel Sahara proposed a short-term engagement to Marlene Dietrich, the figure mentioned was thirty thousand dollars. Dietrich accepted, and began at once to prepare her act and her wardrobe. She contacted Jean Louis, chief dress designer for Columbia studios, and told him she wanted a costume of 'furs, spangles and diamonds'. Fifteen seamstresses worked for three months on the

dresses—'there were actually three gowns,' Jean Louis recalls—
tearing them apart and putting them together as she suggested
alterations. Each dress had two hundred rhinestones—at a dollar
a rhinestone.

When the dress was finally made, Dietrich was photographed
in it, and her little grandson, John Peter, saw the picture. 'Missy
looks just like a Christmas tree,' he said.

Her appearance at the Hotel Sahara caused a sensation. Pictures of the dress were wired round the world, and reporters
described it as 'transparent'. But Marlene considered the description, and the photographs, misleading. 'It was not transparent,'
she insisted. 'Those flash-bulb shots—they shoot right through
a black sweater.' But her protest was ignored, and people came to
Las Vegas—some of them flew from considerable distances—especially to see the dress, and to hear Marlene sing the familiar songs.
Other cabaret offers were not long in coming, but Dietrich did
not accept any of them at once. With her astute business sense,
she knew the value of making people wait.

Finally she accepted an engagement at London's Café de Paris,
at a salary reputed to be £2,000 a week.

The Café de Paris, which received a direct hit from a bomb during the war, was now firmly re-established as a favourite night
club of the 'Four Hundred'. The publicity preceding Dietrich's
arrival was feverish, and within a few hours of the first announcement of her season, the first-night table plan was solidly booked.
Places continued at a premium, in fact, throughout the run. Noël
Coward had written a special introduction for her, and different
celebrities were to pay public tribute to her each night.

Her arrival—she was met by Coward and escorted to the Dorchester—and subsequent Press reception was, as one journalist
described it, worthy of an empress. One would have thought
that a member of the Royal Family was due to arrive if one didn't
already know that the members of the British royal family would

not tolerate the kind of chi-chi that attended Dietrich when she swept down the stairs to face a huge crowd of newspaper people . . .

It turned out to be no more than wishful thinking. Dietrich announced that not only did she expect London to approve her rhinestone dress, but that she had made it even more closely fitting for her début at the Café de Paris. ('She's going to leave no rhinestone unturned,' one wit remarked.) On the evening of the 21st June 1954, she arrived with Coward as uniformed policemen sought to control the crowds that had gathered round the building. Shortly after midnight the dance floor was cleared, and after Coward's doggerel introduction, Marlene stepped into a pink spotlight. 'Something very like the Hampden Roar hit her on mid-stairs,' a journalist reported afterwards. She smiled, kissed Coward, and sang for forty minutes—*Lazy Afternoon, See What the Boys in the Back Room Will Have, I'm the Laziest Gal in Town*, ending, as might be expected, with *Falling in Love Again*. With that number, perhaps the most evocative song of the twenties, she triumphantly finished—nearly a quarter of a century after she first sang it. The reception was rapturous, and the critics added their tributes next day.

On subsequent evenings, other celebrities succeeded Noël Coward with an introductory prologue. They included Richard Todd, Michael Redgrave—who performed a song of homage composed by himself; Donald Wolfit, who quoted an appropriate sonnet by Shakespeare; David Nixon, Herbert Lom, then starring in *The King and I*, whose opening was inadvertently ungallant—'When I was a little boy in Vienna, Marlene Dietrich was a famous star'; Van Johnson, Laurence Harvey, and Robert Morley, who seemed to be unduly long-winded in the process—Dietrich, waiting in the wings for her entrance, was heard to comment: 'Has he forgotten I'm on the bill as well?'

The audience was equally distinguished each night, ranging

from Princess Margaret to the Oliviers, and there were a few guests specially invited by Marlene herself: Sir Alexander Fleming, the Spolianskys, who brought Robert Sherwood as a guest—he was observed to hold his Adam's apple between finger and thumb at the end of the performance, and remark: 'She hasn't got much here, has she?'—and Joan and Neville Smallwood, whom the star remembered with characteristic generosity. Joan Smallwood remembers that, a few days after the performance, Dietrich's maid rang to ask why they had not visited the star back-stage. Joan protested that she had thought Marlene must be too busy, she had heard that there was always a queue of famous people outside her dressing-room after a performance, but the maid had instructions to invite her again and to insist that she and her husband went round afterwards.

In fact, after the show, there was the usual queue outside Marlene's door, including 'several handsome males', but when Joan Smallwood called out her name Marlene came to the door, threw out her arms in greeting, noticed the waiting males and laughed. 'Let the dukes wait, darling,' she said. 'Come in!'

A similar story is told about Alan Fairley, a director of the Café de Paris, who was entertaining the late Cecil McGivern, then a director of BBC television, one evening. Fairley thought that McGivern would like to meet the star, and took him round to her dressing-room. Kenneth Tynan, then dramatic critic of *The Observer*, a new friend of Marlene's, was waiting outside the door. Dietrich came to the threshold, whisked out a hand, pulled Tynan inside and closed the door. McGivern did not meet her that night.

During her London season, Dietrich also carried out a few personal appearances. She had a glittering success at Noël Coward's charity show, *Night of a Hundred Stars*, walking on to the stage like an uncrowned queen, and she also went with him to a Garden Party in Regent's Park, in aid of the Sunshine Home for Blind Babies. Marlene was photographed holding a little boy in her arms and planting a kiss on his left cheek, but during the afternoon tripped over a lighting cable on the lawn and broke two toes of her left foot. She was obliged to wear odd shoes for a week or two, but by the time of an important dress show—at which Coward was also present, wearing a pink cowboy-type shirt and white buckskin shoes, and was presented with a bottle of scent which seemed, as one newspaper remarked, 'to puzzle him a little'—her footwear matched again.

Towards the end of her season, Marlene attended a luncheon to launch a nation-wide 'People against Polio' campaign. She sat in the company of eminent doctors and scientists, including Lord Webb-Johnston, and Lord Mancroft. After drawing her audience's attention to the claims of an obscure doctor in America who had shown impressive results in his efforts to cure polio, Marlene addressed some remarks to the mothers of Britain:

'You should panic more easily when your child gets a cold— it *could* be the first symptoms of infantile paralysis. If a mother lets her child go to school with what appears to be a cold, but is really polio, the child might die or be crippled for life. If she calls a doctor right away he might catch it in time. That is what I mean when I say a mother should panic.'

The medical profession, Dietrich considered, did not altogether share her alarm. Lord Mancroft, speaking later, commented courteously: 'We should not foster the idea that a child with a chill automatically has polio. Equally, it is most important not to allow the present indifference to continue.'

At that moment, Dietrich was observed to be studying the menu.

During her last London week, the newspapers were full of the story of a woman called Hella Christofis, who had been found murdered. Her mother-in-law was suspected of the crime, and charges against her were expected shortly. The dead woman's husband was Christopher, a waiter at the Café de Paris, who had been left with a family of small children to look after.

Without any publicity, Dietrich visited Christopher and made him a generous gift of money.

On her last night at the Café de Paris, she presented all those associated with her appearance there with gifts ranging from a bottle of whisky to a pair of diamond and pearl cuff-links. Then, early in August, she flew to Paris.

CHAPTER TWENTY-SEVEN

Definitions

From Paris, Marlene travelled to the French Riviera, to appear in cabaret at the Sporting Club de Monte Carlo. Here she was the star of a production called *La Nuit d'Août*, a gala charity presentation in aid of the United French Polio Funds. She appeared in the famous open air ballroom, facing the Mediterranean, in her famous Las Vegas gown, and was introduced to an audience of fifteen hundred by Jean Marais. The French actor recited a prologue to her appearance written by Jean Cocteau, who had hoped to declaim it in person but was unfortunately prevented from doing so by illness.

'Marlene Dietrich,' the prologue began, 'your name begins with a caress . . . You wear feathers and furs that seem to belong to your body like furs belong to the animals and feathers to the birds. Your voice, your looks, are those of a Lorelei. But Lorelei was dangerous. You are not dangerous because the secret of your beauty is the secret of your heart . . .'

And it ended: 'Ladies and Gentlemen—from the *paillettes* of *The Blue Angel* to the gown of *Morocco*, from the little black dress in *X-27** to the feathers in *Shanghai Express*, from the diamonds in *Desire* to the wartime American uniform . . . Here to the cliffs of Monaco she comes tonight, like a Chinese fish, a rare bird, the truly unbelievable: a wonderful woman, a true friend of France—Marlene Dietrich!'

Dietrich gave the sophisticated Riviera audience a cosmopoli-

---

* French title for *Dishonoured*.

tan evening of songs—*La Vie en Rose* in French, a German number from *The Blue Angel*, *Lazy Afternoon* in American. It seemed
to love them all.

In October 1954, Dietrich made her second appearance in Las
Vegas, and an observant newsman from the *Los Angeles Times*
commented that her new costume revealed that 'there were no
surgical scars in the midriff vicinity of the alluring screen star . . .
One could also detect the presence of a mole neighbouring her
right hip.' She made her entrance in a diaphanous costume and
sang *Look Me Over Closely*, during which a wind machine caused
the skirt to billow interestingly. As a result of this, she signed a
two-year contract with the management, specifying one four-week
engagement per year at a fee of a hundred thousand dollars.
Marlene announced that this engagement, with a similar one for
the Café de Paris, completed her cabaret plans for 1955 and 1956.

After Las Vegas she resumed life in her Manhattan apartment,
entertaining friends and also publishing a series of magazine
articles entitled *How to be Loved*. She offered the following advice to female readers:

'To make a man happy is a full-time job—with no holidays.

'It leaves us very little time to take ourselves too seriously.
And if you have children you have no time at all. Or you should
have no time at all. The more plentiful the work, the less time to
be neurotic. And when the work is directed towards the making
and the keeping of a happy home, it makes you rich in contentment and puts occupational afflictions like aching bones into the
only place where they belong—a hot bath (if you have time before your man comes home, that is).

'This rich contentment will make you do a lot of things you
had forgotten. You will remember your instincts' aerial, the tender fine antennae you used to stretch his way in the beginning.

Although neglected, they are still with you, dusty and bent—but you can straighten them.

'With your antennae back at work, life should be easy. They'll tell you many things. His desires of each day and night, and his dislikes. When to be quiet, when to talk, when to give an opinion on his problems and when just to listen, when to ask questions on how his work is going and when to wait until he wants to think of work and talk about it. When to welcome him with kisses, and when your hand in his for just a moment is quite enough.'

All this reminds one of von Sternberg's remark: 'She is the most thoughtful person I have ever met in my life . . .'

As a result of these articles, journalists began making a compendium of what they termed 'Dietrich Definitions and Viewpoints'. They revealed the star as an interesting mixture of fatalist and iconoclast.

GLAMOUR: 'Glamour, in a word, is assurance. It is a kind of knowing that you are all right in every way, mentally and physically and in appearance, and that, whatever the occasion or the situation, you are equal to it. That feeling a woman gets when she has on a new outfit is something akin to glamour. When others gather from your poise, appearance and command of yourself, that you have that inner assurance, you become glamorous in their eyes.'

SUCCESS: 'Success in life depends upon your sense of values.'

MONEY: 'It *does* bring happiness, if used wisely, and don't let anyone tell you it doesn't. If I had lots of money now, I'd fill hundreds of boats with food for Europe's starving children. That would bring happiness to them—and to me!'

PREJUDICES: 'Prejudices are wrong ideas which have been handed on to us and which we hand on to our children, thus keeping alive a long list of historical errors. We should teach our children fundamentals and principles; that honesty is the best policy, that knowledge is power, and so on, with special stress on the Golden Rule—then we should let the poor kids invent their own prejudices, if they must have some!'

MEN: 'In general, men are better people than women. They have stronger characters, better brains, and are not so muddled in their thinking.'

PATRIOTISM: 'Real patriotism means you have selected the particular part of the earth towards which you will be loyal, and where you expect to work out your destiny by doing your part to make that particular spot the most civilised, the most cultured and the happiest part on the globe. Since I became an American citizen by naturalisation, I have become more aware of the power of patriotism.'

FREEDOM: 'You really become free when you are happily adjusted to life. Inner freedom, that freeing of the spirit from the bondage of unhealthy thinking and fear, is harder to achieve than physical freedom, or the right to roam around where you please.'

DRUDGERY: 'I was asked if I ever scrub the floor at my home. Why, of course! Why not? I don't mind doing anything if there is a good reason for it—and I do like good clean floors.'

CHILDREN: 'We owe it to God as a debt for having been permitted to become parents, to see that our children are better than we—better citizens, better human beings. If they are not, then the world stands still. All the progress and hope of the world lies in its children.'

LOVE: 'What is love? If you've never known it, you wouldn't understand it if it were explained to you. If you have known it, you don't need a definition from me . . . Love is something you shouldn't try to think about, anyway. Like faith, it's something noble and grand and far beyond the reach of our reasoning why or wherefore.'

Dietrich on Life was popular, and she was constantly being offered large sums of money to write. The magazine that published her first series (and paid her twenty thousand dollars for them) had suggested that she might like a writer to work with her, but she declined. As usual, her attitude was rigorously professional. 'Writing,' she explained, 'is easy—easier than singing and acting.' Then a note of weariness crept in, 'I really don't want to write, or to make movies, or to sing. I have no ambition. I work because I need the money. I wish I didn't have to work. I lead a full life— and not working would give me more time for it.'

But work, as she said, was necessary, and she also began a new radio programme at this time, *A Time for Love*. It was based on her own idea of her role as Lola-Lola, and she supervised the whole series, hiring the artists and writers, signing the cheques. She rejected television offers, however, as she felt uncertain of the medium; though she seriously considered for a while a proposal that she should play Lady Jane Bigby, who became the consort of a Syrian sheik—one of the several women who found romance in the Orient in Lesley Blanch's *The Wilder Shores of Love*. After some discussion, she decided not to land on those particular shores.

Meanwhile, in London, her appearance at the Café de Paris was formally commemorated. The management ordered a dedicatory plaque, which was affixed to the column against which the star had leaned to take her applause. A party was given in December 1954 for the unveiling of its simple legend:

DIETRICH RESTED HERE.

CHAPTER TWENTY-EIGHT

Zuleika

The lady and the legend were back again in London late in May 1955; and neither, as usual, seemed a day older. Contracted for a second season at the Café de Paris, at a salary of £6,000 a week, Marlene Dietrich faced the waiting reporters with her usual ironic assurance. The following remarks were recorded.

To girls: 'Buy the book I'm writing—it explains everything about boys. It says—no, buy it yourself and see.' To British fathers she mysteriously advised: 'Stay away from the gaming tables.' And to mothers: 'Don't give advice to your daughters—they'll find their way just as well without it.' The elegant, world-weary accents were unchanged; the only difference to be noted, in fact, was that the *femme fatale's* skirt was displaying just one inch more leg than fashion dictated.

Prior to her arrival, Danny Kaye had been occupying the famous apartment designed by Oliver Messel on the roof of the Dorchester Hotel (25 guineas a day). Dietrich had instructed her London manager that she wanted the Messel suite, and Mr Kaye was accordingly asked if he would give it up in favour of Miss Dietrich. He would, of course, and did. And, settling in amidst vases of flowers sent by admirers, 'I am spoiled for ever,' the star smokily confessed. 'This is *the* most wonderful town, *the* most wonderful audiences . . .' While she was talking to a reporter the phone rang. It was Danny Kaye himself.

'Yes, my love,' she said. 'And I want to thank you very much— you're an angel. It was like coming home.' *Like coming home.* A 25-guinea-a-day flat.

About her fabulous salary, she had this to say: 'This cabaret season is for love. My other work is for the loot. For love, dear boy—just to sing to people. I make no money. It all goes in taxes . . .'

In the days that followed, Dietrich prepared for her Café de Paris act—the wispy chiffon gowns, copied from those she wore at her last Las Vegas opening, were brought out of trunks, and René, the Mayfair hairdresser who attends Princess Margaret, was summoned; visited old friends; and agreed to perform in Noël Coward's *Night of a Hundred Stars*.

Her opening night was celebrity-packed, the audience ranging from Clifton Webb to the Sultan of Johore, Christopher Fry to Tyrone Power, Leslie Caron to Emlyn Williams. Incomparably poised, resting against the pillar with an inscribed plaque commemorating that she had rested there before, Dietrich acknowledged her ovation with the familiar, enigmatic half-smile. She came forward slowly, in her wrapping of flesh-coloured chiffon, and the immaculate Douglas Fairbanks Jnr delivered an introductory peroration specially written by Christopher Fry.

She sang all her old favourites. Then, at the end, she drew a trick from her sleeve. With wild Cockney accents, dipped in Berlinese, she sang *Knocked 'em in the Old Kent Road*. Shocked into vigorous and persistent applause, the audience encouraged her to sing chorus after chorus while a pink spotlight caught the famous rhinestones on her dress.

Then the management announced that each night during her season she would be introduced by a celebrated woman—Lady Violet Bonham Carter, Eva Bartok, Dame Edith Evans, Viscountess Tarbat, and Mrs Bessie Braddock, whom Dietrich was later to salute 'as one working girl to another'. A few prominent males, such as Orson Welles, Jack Hawkins and Robert Morley, were also to be allowed to do the honours.

Next day the papers did battle over her. 'Fame clings to Die-

trich like a skin-tight gown,' one critic wrote. 'Last night she retained her queenship of cabaret.' This, indeed, seemed to be the
majority opinion. London, via the Old Kent Road, was Dietrich's
again.

How did it go, having these famous people introduce her?

It was marvellous, it was ludicrous, it ranged from pathos to
bathos.

Lady Violet Bonham Carter, later Lady Asquith, introduced
her charmingly. She recalled the time when Marlene Dietrich
entertained the troops in the war, and allowed herself to be sawn
in half by Orson Welles.

'How terrible,' said Lady Asquith, 'that one should be called
upon to select which half of the lovely Marlene to retain.'

There was a roar of appreciation from the audience.

The choice of Bessie Braddock, the Liverpool MP, to introduce Marlene Dietrich caused unexpected bad feeling.

On the night that the rotund Mrs Braddock did the honours,
Lady Docker, a social favourite, was in the audience. She seemed
surprised that someone had arranged for the Liverpool MP to
appear in this unusual role. It has been suggested that she took
exception to the order of precedence, but the situation passed off
without real incident or embarrassment.

Bessie. Bessie Braddock. This extraordinary, solidly-built MP
from Liverpool. Why on earth had she been asked to introduce a
star of screen and stage—Marlene Dietrich? It didn't make sense.
Or did it? The atmosphere surrounding their first meeting gave
way to a friendship which blossomed strangely. So much so that,
ten years later, Bessie Braddock was saying lightly: 'Marlene.
Oh. We meet on and off over the years. We're great friends, you
know.'

Well. This was the awkward beginning of the friendship.
There was Marlene. Slick as only a talented actress can be. Every
hair in place. The eyes just so. The mouth, poised, half open.

143

The head inclined just so, to catch the light. Oh, we know about lights. The hair again. That iridescent hair. The costume, dazzling. The movements, provocative. And into this world, into the ring, steps Bessie Braddock. Can you imagine it?

The night-club-goers laughed as they saw the big woman stand beside the star. But Mrs Braddock can take that sort of thing. She stood the fire and made the introduction.

And what did Miss Dietrich have to say?

She looked at the badges that Mrs Braddock always wears in her lapel. 'What are they?' she asked with a trace of amusement in her voice.

'This is the Labour Party badge, and this one is the Union of Shop, Distributive and Allied Workers.'

'And this one,' said Miss Dietrich, with a visible raising of the eyebrows.

Mrs Braddock, well rehearsed, touched the badge which showed a design of a boxer with raised fists. 'I'm Honorary President of the Professional Boxers' Association.'

'Really,' said Miss Dietrich, her eyebrows now at the apex of surprise. 'How charming.'

Mrs Braddock made a good job of the introduction and putting down her orange juice—she's a teetotaller—she told the glamorous West End audience that she had accepted the invitation for two reasons. To acknowledge Miss Dietrich's work for the Forces in the war (loud cheers) and to foster Anglo-American relations (more cheers).

'I very seldom find myself in the company I am in tonight. But I intend as a reciprocal arrangement to ask Miss Dietrich along to the House of Commons.'

How they all clapped! They clapped so loud and so long they nearly ruined Miss Dietrich's entrance.

Mrs Braddock was true to her word. There was a Zuleika Dobson quality about her visit to the House of Commons. That serious political commentator Walter Terry searched his soul for suitable words to describe the occasion. 'Awe-struck MPs, intent on a good old row in the Commons, stopped dead in their tracks and gaped,' he wrote.

It was the week after Bessie Braddock had introduced her at the Café de Paris. Mrs Braddock arranged the lunch in the Strangers' dining-room as an all-party affair, afraid that there might be some jealousy if it was kept solely within Labour Party limits. She may have been right. MPs queued to be introduced. It was a simple meal—hors d'œuvres, sole, strawberries and cream. After it, she was taken to the Speaker's gallery to watch Question Time. She sat looking over the Socialist benches, the Tories below her, and sitting there in head-hugging cream hat sweeping low over her eyes, she was a magnet to all the politicians' glances. 'The sunlight shafting across the Commons,' wrote one observant commentator of the scene, 'played on the knees of the miraculous Marlene.'

The Opposition of the day, Clem Attlee and Herbert Morrison, prominent on the Front Bench, were preparing for a heavy and serious debate, the most formidable of a new session. Another scribe said: 'Her impact could be reckoned as stupendous and equally damaging to all parties, as from the gallery her languorous eyes glanced in turn on both the Front Benches, the Speaker, and the women MPs dressed in their summer dresses.'

Then the Questions began, as Opposition spokesmen tested the Government, and the Government replied.

Marlene listened raptly. She listened as Miss Jennie Lee asked the Colonial Secretary about the problem of unemployment and immigration in Jamaica, and the state of the arrowroot industry in the island of St Vincent.

It was something quite out of Miss Dietrich's range of interests and she could have been forgiven if she had let her mind wander. Did the Colonial Secretary know, asked Jennie Lee, that the planters in St Vincent were shockingly badly paid? That there was an American agency which had a double monopoly in arrowroot? That there was shocking profiteering? Frank Allaun pressed the Colonial Secretary further, and asked for details of wages on arrowroot estates.

'Men earn between 22s 6d a week and 34s a week, women rather less,' said Mr Henry Hopkinson. 'And there is no special provision during periods of unemployment.'

Emmanuel Shinwell joined in the debate: 'How can we justify a colonial policy when such disgraceful wages are being paid?"

Marlene left soon after this, missing the opportunity of hearing a promising politician launching an attack on Peter Thorneycroft, then President of the Board of Trade. It was the Member for Huyton—Mr Harold Wilson.

What she had heard made a big impression on Marlene. The procession, the Speaker entering the chamber solemnly in his robes to start the day's business. 'I love all this tradition,' she said. But she loved the debate too. 'I was struck by the quality and fierceness of the debate. I've learnt something about arrowroot today. I'll have to find out more.'

The car to take her away had been ordered for three o'clock. It was nearly five before she left, excited and delighted and fascinated by what she had seen. And leaving behind a newly-won audience into the bargain.

The Café de Paris season which launched her again into cabaret (though this is not how she likes to describe this work) was a glorious success.

She created a sensation by attending the Rose of England Ball at the Dorchester Hotel. The money was for Gosfield Hall, a charity, and naturally when they got Marlene there, everyone called upon her to sing. 'Sing?' she said. 'I am sorry, but I cannot because of the terms of my contract.' But she wanted to help, and the solution was far more dramatic and exciting for the few who could afford it. She agreed to be auctioned as a dancing partner. She could have been content to dance only once, or a couple of dances at the most. But not the professional Marlene. Once she puts her mind to a thing, she does it wholeheartedly and thoroughly. She had no fewer than a dozen partners, raising several thousand pounds. One partner paid £500, the highest, for the privilege of dancing with the legend.

Several weeks later Marlene Dietrich sang before the Queen and the Duke of Edinburgh at a private party given by Lord Astor in Upper Grosvenor Street. Not only were the Queen and Prince Philip there, but guests included Princess Margaret, Princess Alexandra, and a host of titled people closest to the throne. The Queen got a seat on the sofa with the Duke—but many were content to sit on the floor. And audiences don't come much more select than that.

CHAPTER TWENTY-NINE

I am Marlene Dietrich

The film star chrysalis had grown into the gorgeous butterfly of a world star entertainer, an entertainer in her own right. This meant many changes. Of course she did make more films, but not in the same mould. It meant changes in personality, changes at any rate in the personality that the public saw. Interviews became franker and franker. She had trained herself to present a certain image, but many were the times when, tired after world travel, exhausted by her own demanding standards, she would arrive at an airport to be faced by a barrage of questions. They would ask her about being a grandmother. About her American citizenship. About her earnings and about the cost of her clothes. Small wonder she would sometimes answer back snappily. But where the private person and the public image in Marilyn Monroe merged into a tragically schizophrenic creature, Dietrich has always had her escape valves. Like the occasion when she arrived at Orly airport, Paris, to sing in a European tour—the overture, in fact, to her first singing engagement in her native Germany.

It was an irritable Marlene Dietrich who arrived after the transatlantic journey with some nineteen pieces of luggage, at the end of 1959.

Photographers pressed her to pose with Bruno Coquatrix, the impresario arranging this first post-war appearance in France.

'Kiss him,' they urged.

'Why should I?' she rapped. 'I don't know him.'

All around the French magazine photographers were up to their antics, pushing, shoving, lying down in ridiculous poses to snatch shots of her. French and English reporters clutching soiled note-books pressed against her; microphones were pushed at her; questions were shouted from all directions. 'This is ridiculous,' she hissed. 'There are far too many people. Far, far too many people.'

The reporters were insistent.

'What songs are you going to sing in Paris?'

'Come and hear me and you'll find out.'

'How do you like Paris?'

'I haven't seen it yet.'

'Would you name the ten most attractive men in the world?'

She gave the questioner a withering look. 'I find those sort of questions really *too* old-fashioned.'

It wasn't a very pleasant welcome, and as a result she was re-luctant to see any more Press. To requests for interviews she shrugged: 'From now on it's work, work, work. I'm not going to be tempted out to dinner or nightspots until after my première. And if I'm not allowed to rehearse in peace, I shall ask for the protec-tion of the gendarmes.'

This was the European tour that really established her as one of the great entertainers of all time. It was four years after her fabulous season at London's Café de Paris.

What had happened in the meantime? For one thing, her husband Rudolf Sieber had been ill in California, and was in a Hollywood hospital after a heart attack. In a flash she was at his side, and spent hours in the hospital daily until he came through. He was nursed back to health, and not until he returned to his chicken farm did she relax. Mr Sieber, who had been playing such a quiet role in the background, commented: 'She's a regular guy.' Years later he was asked about their marriage arrangements, he with his chicken farm in California, she with her home in New York. It was all right, he said. They were good friends. He wouldn't like to be among the theatre set. 'I'm a shy man. I don't like the limelight.'

Later in 1956 she agreed to play opposite Vittorio de Sica, the Italian film star and producer, in a film to be made in Monte Carlo. 'Why?' she said with characteristic charm. 'I chose him because he is the most romantic middle-aged man in the world.'

The film was called *The Monte Carlo Story*. Her presence in the principality was not without some drama. There was the occasion when she turned up at the Monte Carlo Casino wearing a £500 outfit of black silk slacks and silver-spangled jacket, and was turned away from the private rooms, since women in trousers were forbidden. Aristotle Onassis was supposed to have explained to her later that it was rather an old-fashioned rule, but it was a rule.

Certainly Miss Dietrich was in no mood to discuss the matter the next day.

It was during the making of this film that there was another 'misunderstanding' with the Press. A Press conference was called in Rome to promote the film, and co-star Natalie Trundy was there, a very pretty sixteen-year-old starlet—who in fact was highly praised for her performance. Miss Trundy, whose youth may have made her over-sensitive, returned to the States afterwards and reported 'She never spoke to me. At the Press conference in Rome photographers asked her to pose with me. Miss Dietrich walked away.'

On her birthday, Miss Trundy said, de Sica gave the young starlet a huge bunch of baby orchids. 'Miss Dietrich didn't even offer me any good wishes.' The story sounds untypical of Marlene Dietrich.

It was a moody Dietrich who met the Press during these days. Perhaps because film publicity was taking her back to the world she had just left. When she was asked the traditional question about being a glamorous grandmother, she could stand it no longer. 'Grandmother, grandmother, always that word grandmother. Do grandmothers have to go around on crutches . . . ?'

The film came out the following year. Cecil Wilson, one of her great admirers, said: 'Never did I expect to be bored by the combined beauties of Monte Carlo and Marlene Dietrich, but the impossible happened.'

The Monte Carlo Story was a mild comedy about a poor marquise searching for a wealthy husband. She finds him conveniently at the gaming tables—or so she thinks. Each is drawn to the other by imagining the other's wealth, which turns out to be nonexistent. But, ah, beneath it all, they find True Love. 'As genuine,' said Mr Wilson, 'as any love can be in an artificial picture which is all icing and no cake.'

But Mr Wilson reserved special words for the lady herself. 'Miss Dietrich, carved in inflammable stone, weighing up the world with parted lips and half-closed eyes, and wearing dresses that practically immobilise her, remains a wonder to behold. Otherwise, beyond making her sing *Back Home Again in Indiana* in her uncompromisingly Middle-European accent, or leaning her up against a pillar to croon a French song in the most seductive tenor that ever emerged from woman's lips, the film asks little of her durable allure.'

But while the film was going out on the circuits, Miss Dietrich was returning to her new love—cabaret. Or what she later said was not 'cabaret', but 'playing theatres'.

At Las Vegas she wore a dress that beat any yet. A gown which contained two hundred and twenty-seven thousand hand-sewn beads which had taken six months to make, the result of no less than a million stitches. The twelve-foot train was made from the breast feathers of three hundred swans. Later when she appeared for a brief part in the master-showman Mike Todd's spendiferous *Round the World in Eighty Days*, it was said that her costume cost £20,000 to make. It didn't.

Marlene Dietrich has never, never underestimated the importance of clothes. The man who said of her 'Fame clings to her like a skin-tight dress' coined a brilliant description. Skin-tight indeed. 'I never use undies,' she said provocatively. 'They ruin a good tight-fitting dress.'

To listen to Dietrich on the subject of dress might startle some of today's young stars who think it's enough to throw something pretty on. For herself, she admitted recently, she'd be happy to wear jeans. In fact, she's quite often been seen at rehearsals in men's jeans. She startled Sidney's women, who of course are startled by almost anything, by walking about their city in jeans.

Her reasoning is simple. People pay to see her well dressed, and it is part of the act. So when she dresses she approaches the subject with the same incredible professionalism as she does the rest of the business of entertaining.

Madame Ginette Spanier, director of a Paris fashion house, records what it's like to be at the receiving end. 'She is one of the most fastidious dressers in the world. Anyone who has had any experience of dressing Marlene Dietrich knows that when she says "I'll take it" that's when the trouble begins. Once when we had remade the lining of a jacket for her six times, I finally could not control myself any longer. I said, "Look, the film public is going to look at you and your legs. They're not going to notice a pleat on the right side of your bust. And if they do, the film will be a flop anyway." "Ah," said Marlene, "but if in twenty years' time my daughter should supervise a reshowing of my films she would notice the pleat and think Mother had lost her touch there." I had no answer to that and redid the lining for the seventh time.'

On another occasion she talked about her clothes to *The Observer* newspaper, whose interviewer found her in a little black dress, by Balenciaga, and a wild mink coat. The little black dress, the interviewer observed, was 'littler and subtler than volumes of *Vogue* could imply.'

What Miss Dietrich had to say about dressing was truly revealing. 'I dress for the image,' she announced. 'Not for myself, not for the public, not for fashion, not for men. When I played in *The Blue Angel* people really thought that was me. They really thought that was me. If I dressed myself I wouldn't bother at all. Clothes bore me. I'd wear jeans. I adore them. I get them in a public store. Men's, of course. I can't remember when I last got a new pair. They last so long, and get better and better. But I dress for the profession. I've had clothes *made* for me because of my unusual shape, broad shoulders, narrow hips. Of course, if I am with someone who I know wants to show me off, then I dress so that they can show me off. I dress according to what I am doing—that is what *taste* is—and to suit the country I am in. In Paris you can be more crazy. New York is a practical place. I adore Paris. I have never made a mistake. I don't remember not having confidence. Mistakes are not necessary because I can see if something goes wrong during the making. And I can stop it.'

She was asked about her fur coat.

'This one isn't mine. I have no fur coats. To buy a fur coat for £10,000 I must earn at least ten times as much tax, you know. Who cares? Balenciaga sent it over.'

Her uneasy relations with the Press had been broken by this triumphant 1959 success in Paris. The sleuths who had hunted her at airports were a different breed from the reviewers who became stage-door Johnnies besieging her dressing-room after the shows.

The pseudonymous Paul Tanfield was there in Paris to mark the first night, her first appearance in Paris since the war. He conveyed some of the magic which Marlene Dietrich never fails to spin when she steps on to a stage.

'She swayed to the microphone,' he began in his late-night despatch, 'with that lubricated walk which is as old as Eve. Her hair a cascade of spun gold. Her dress fitting closer than close. Her figure like a débutante's. Age, Shakespeare said, cannot wither

her. He was speaking of Cleopatra; the same goes for Marlene. Dietrich, the soignée, indestructible fifty-four-year-old butterfly. A grandmother, and that rarity, a legend in her own time.'

It was a star-spangled night at L'Étoile, with the Begum Aga Khan, Martine Carol, Lena Horne, Maurice Chevalier, Jean Cocteau and many old friends to cheer in the audience. Afterwards she went on to a party with Yves St Laurent, the fashion designer. Princess Margaret's hairdresser, René, was again in attendance, staying three days to do her hair. 'It was nothing,' he said with a shrug. 'I once flew to Monte Carlo to do her hair for a charity ball.'

Miss Dietrich could afford such luxuries. The bill for her two-week appearance at L'Étoile was £30,000.

Nancy Spain met her for the first time after seeing this performance and was greatly struck by the star. As she went into Marlene's dressing-room, Marlene looked up at Nancy Spain and said: 'Oh, you've pinched my jacket.'

'It doesn't look at all like yours,' said the journalist.

'No. I've taken out the red lining and put a white lining into mine, otherwise we might well be twins.'

Twins! Nancy Spain gasped at the idea. She was completely won over, and Miss Dietrich gave her the rare chance of a lengthy interview the next day.

It was 11.30 am when she answered the door to Miss Spain without make-up, hair hanging over her eyes, dressed in a pale blue gown of angora with satin facings. She drew Miss Spain into the room almost conspiratorially. 'I have managed to scrape a little hole here among the roses,' she said, indicating the jungle of flowers, small trees and shrubs—presents from admirers—which enveloped the room. Some of them were fading somewhat, and Marlene looked at them with apparent concern. 'They need aspirin. There is a rose over there that needs aspirin very badly.'

They talked of clothes and beauty and men, and Miss Spain was impressed by her beauty. 'Completely natural beauty. I promise you, she has never had her face lifted. She has never had a massage, and frankly is at her best in disarray.'

That is a view supported by all her friends. Michael Wilding said of her with admiration: 'Soap and water, a dab of lipstick, a touch of powder and a few minutes with a mascara brush is all I've known her to use. Ten minutes from start to finish. When Marlene says she'll be ready in ten minutes, she means exactly that. She washes her hair under the shower.'

Talking to Nancy Spain of men, she repeated what she had said before in different ways. And especially of great men. The Flemings (penicillin, not Bond!), the Hemingways, the Faulkners, the Goethes, and so on. Her humility was striking. She told Miss Spain of the time Sir John Gielgud was playing in New York. 'I climbed up the gallery stairs, away from the stuffed shirts —I was up there with the students. It was wonderful. We shouted and yelled.'

Her success at L'Étoile for which she had so obviously keyed herself up, and the pleasant way in which Nancy Spain had restored her confidence in the Press, caused her to unbend and it opened a new era in her public life. From then on, to serious interviewers whom she felt she could trust, Marlene Dietrich was a lamb.

One of the first to meet the new Marlene was Robert Muller, former dramatic critic, writer, playwright. He captured in a unique way the flavour of her speech.

'Listen,' she told him bluntly, 'I live by the law of demand and supply. They want me to do this singing thing. All right, I sing. They want me to do a film. All right, I do a film.

'People ask me what makes me tick. It's all demand and supply. If people want money from me, I give 'em money. If they need advice, I give 'em advice. If they want shelter, I give 'em shelter. If they want to be seen with me, I let 'em be seen with me. That's my method. If they didn't ask me, I wouldn't go anywhere. There is probably some country where they say, "Dietrich—who the hell is she?" Well, I wouldn't go there. Everyone's had this grandmother publicity stuffed down their throats for so long, they think I'm ancient.'

Back to men again, she observed: 'I've always been attracted to intelligent men. I can pick 'em in a full room, just like that. I don't care what age they are.'

Again the humility. 'If I have one regret it's that I would like to have done something more valuable with my life. Something for humanity. A doctor or a chemist, you know. After all, what have I done? "The pictures you have given us and all that." I'm replaceable. But can Dr Salk or Fleming be replaced?'

A fortnight later there was not much evidence of her humility, however. She left Paris for the States with some fifty-one pieces of luggage and was charged £600 excess baggage. 'How dare they,' she said. 'I don't see why I should pay. I am Marlene Dietrich.'

CHAPTER THIRTY

A *Slavonic Soul*

Her success in Paris paved the way for her first tour of Germany in May the following year. It was a visit she faced with some apprehension. She would agree to tour West Germany but not East Germany. No, not even when they offered her £1,700 a day to sing in East Berlin.

To West Berlin she did go. Nearly two thousand people turned up to give her a great ovation with Mayor Willy Brandt in attendance. It was a marvellous tour, and a brave one. She had to face such embarrassments as the 17-year-old girl who ran out to her car to scream, 'I hate you. You betrayed Germany in the war.' At Bad Kissingen, in spite of a successful stage appearance, there were boos and cat-calls from a street gang. She made her exit by the back door.

In spite of some resentment the tour was a great success, and Germans wanted to know whether they had won back their native Marlene. And Marlene wanted to know if she had won back her native Germany. It was an uneasy truce; not long afterwards Marlene was reaffirming her hatred of everything that represented the Nazi regime. If any Germans still wanted to be associated with that reign of terror, she made it chillingly clear, she wanted no part of it.

A year later she agreed to act in Stanley Kramer's *Judgment at Nuremberg*. She played a German widow.

In 1963 she once again showed by her actions which way her sympathies lay. She accepted from the Belgians an award for services to the Allied cause in the war—Knight of the Leopold Order of Belgium.

A few months later she was singing at the El Alamein reunion, drawing tears from the eyes of old warriors. She sang to the soldiers such songs as *Lili Marlene* and *The Boys in the Back Room*. She said of the war: 'The thing worth remembering is the sharing. Then it was, Share my food, my water, my safety, my danger. Nowadays it's, You've got to hang on to what you've got or it's snatched away from you. Sharing was a positive good which we could practise now.'

For a few magical moments the Desert Rats who watched that eerie, lovely face caught in the spotlights, wondered if the war too hadn't been some beautiful, wonderful emotional experience, and not a bloody slaughter, a tragedy of mixed boredom and pain.

The Queen Mother was there, and Monty addressed the five thousand old campaigners. Vera Lynn sang *A Nightingale sang in Berkeley Square*.

Then Marlene Dietrich sang poignantly *Where have all the young men gone? Gone to graveyards every one* . . .

It was, as usual, a superlative performance. A couple of weeks later she was singing in a Royal Variety Show. She was singing with—or against if you like—the Beatles.

How did she react to these youngsters? 'The Beatles? I thought they were wonderful—who doesn't?' A broad-minded view in a year when some of the oldsters regarded the rise of the Beatles on a par with the fall of the British Empire.

She was in great form when she rehearsed with the lads from Liverpool. She was philosophical in recognising that the majority of those who paid the magnificent total of £50,000 to the Variety Artists' Benevolent Fund wanted largely to see the long-haired four. She didn't mind. She lined up with them at rehearsals, and agreed to be photographed. It was great fun on the night, as the Beatles stole the show with their brand of humour. Beatle John

Lennon stepped to the front of the stage and cracked: 'For our next number I want the people in the cheap seats to start clapping. The rest of you can rattle your jewellery.'

There was some disagreement, though, when it came to analysing the television ratings. It was discovered that while the Beatles were appearing, 2,394,000 people in the London area were viewing. When Marlene Dietrich came on, the number shot up to 2,525,000. But it was pointed out that earlier viewers might have been watching an Ingrid Bergman film on the other wavelength while the Beatles were on. Either way, it seemed that Dietrich plus Bergman beat the Beatles into the homesteads.

She told Godfrey Winn, though, what she really felt about young people. 'I feel so sad for them. I don't just mean the ones who play their guitars for a short time, but all the young people. They pour themselves out too quickly. They have affairs almost on first sight. It is considered *de rigueur* now. It's no longer daring, just dull.'

It was success after success. Were there any heights left to scale? Yes, the Edinburgh Festival—who would have thought of that?

Lord Harewood made the announcement. She would appear in August 1964 with a band of twenty under Bert Bacharach. His Lordship pronounced himself 'rather excited' about it. She would appear at the Royal Lyceum Theatre in a late show. The fee? Lord Harewood hedged. 'We are doing all right and so is she.'

The year 1964 was busy and exciting. It was her first series of performances in Russia. Typically she observed after one marvellous ovation: 'I think I have a Russian soul myself.'

It all started when she met a Russian at a cocktail party. He turned out to be a cultural attaché. 'Moscow cannot wait,' he said gallantly.

She made her début in Moscow in May and took thirty curtain calls at the Estradi Theatre. 'All I can do is thank you,' she said in a voice filled with emotion. 'I have loved you for a long time.' At a conservative estimate the applause lasted some forty minutes.

At the end of her stay, a fortnight later, she seemed to have conquered all Russia where Napoleon had failed. The Estradi Theatre, which is directly across the river from the Kremlin, was in uproar, and the audience wouldn't let her leave. They clapped madly. A girl thrust a necklace at her. 'No, I can't take it,' said Marlene, running off the stage and locking herself in her dressing-room. A Russian soldier ran up on the stage, went to her dressing-room, and managed to get her back on stage.

'I thank you for your sings,' he exclaimed.

'My sings? Ah! You are welcome.'

Half an hour after the show had ended not one Russian had left the theatre. They crushed into each other trying to force their way to the stage, tossing up presents for her, great bouquets of flowers. After the thirty-ninth curtain Marlene Dietrich suddenly took her shoes off with one hand, and waved them at the audience while she clasped a big bunch of roses with the other.

She turned to one of her party. 'I've never known anything like this. Every time I loosen my sleeves they think I am going to take my dress off.'

She went forward to the front of the stage, and unzipped the sleeves of her tight sheath dress.

Finally she started introducing the people from her party on the stage. 'This is the man who minds my baggage. This is the man who manages the pretty lights. This is my translator, Nora. This is the Man from the Ministry of Culture.' At this she trotted out across the stage, tugging a reluctant little plump man in an open-neck shirt. The Russians rose to their feet and cheered.

Back in London she talked warmly about the Russians in a way that would melt any cold war. She sat over a vodka, talking of her plans to visit Russia again and told a friend: 'The Russians have a way of being happy and sad. There are no lukewarm emotions. I still have a Slavonic soul.'

After a reception like that the Edinburgh Festival might have come as an anti-climax. But she was being carried on the crest of a wave. Edinburgh was marvellous, the Scots were marvellous. And they paid her the compliment, she said, of buying all the tickets for her show before the tourists could get there. A beautiful city, Edinburgh.

But there were more peaks to scale. *The Times* of London, for example. Critical acclaim from the one British newspaper which stands back at a good distance from these 'entertainer' people.

She toppled *The Times* critic completely. 'What more is there to say about Marlene Dietrich?' he began nostalgically. 'She defies change. To watch her work is a lesson of sheer professionalism. The appearance, of course, is unforgettable: the pencil-slim silhouette sways in a glittering peach-coloured creation which catches the spotlight at every movement; and just about the biggest thing in faces since the Mona Lisa, and she knows it. Few performers have taken more effectively to heart the jumbled injunction: "Don't just do something. Stand there."'

One of her happy memories of the Edinburgh Festival was her meeting the famous Russian pianist, Richter. She was at dinner, and recalls the moment. 'He came to my table and presented me with flowers. Imagine that. I asked him if I could see his hands. They are large and soft. Now *he* is an *artist*. I do not call myself that. On my passport I am described as an actress.'

Having said that, she was to rethink the problem; a little later she was saying she was an artist. She liked Paris, she said, because Paris recognised artists. 'In Paris there is freedom. They let you live and no one bothers you.'

When asked about her cabaret work, she retorted: 'I never play cabaret. I play in theatres. That's quite different. Oh, I did play the Café de Paris and Las Vegas, but that was five years ago.'

Then she decided she was a *chanteuse*, a *diseuse*.

In 1965 she started the year by suing one airline, and went on to feature in the advertisements of another. In January of that year she was suing Air France for the loss of a £2,500 mink coat and other luggage, a sum total of over £3,000. By September she had agreed to pose for British Overseas Airways Corporation, in a bid to point out the excellent facilities for leg room in British jets. It was a gesture which was to rub salt into the old wound with her native fatherland.

But before this occurred an extraordinary book appeared in America, and later in London, considered by some to be critical of the star. *Fun in a Chinese Laundry* was written by no less a person than von Sternberg, and it was a record of his years in Hollywood. The book was widely reviewed in America, and reports coming back from Hollywood surprised Miss Dietrich's friends. The man who made her, it seemed, had revised his opinion of her. He needn't have bothered; she was managing to stand very well on her own two feet. The book appeared on the thirty-fifth anniversary of the first film he made with her. He was now seventy-one. Throughout the book he referred to her as Fräulein, or Frau Dietrich. 'The first to notice if I was looking for a pencil, the first to rush for a chair if I wanted to sit down. Not the slightest resistance was offered to my domination of her performance,' he began. 'Her energy was enormous. She was subject to severe depressions though these were balanced by periods of unbelievable vigour. To exhaust her was not possible. It was she who exhausted others with an enthusiasm few were able to share.'

He went on to say that her attitude to him amounted to a mixture of hero-worship and complete submissiveness. 'A geyser of praise began to shoot from her every hour and on the hour, and there was nothing I could do to avoid being scalded.'

Marlene Dietrich happened to be in London when von Stern-

berg's book was published there in the autumn of 1966. He made
the trip to London to publicise it. A party was given by the
British publishers to launch the book. Miss Dietrich was invited.
The publishers said they hoped she'd be coming.

But Miss Dietrich didn't go. Von Sternberg and his memoirs
had been elegantly dealt with.

CHAPTER THIRTY-ONE

Let's go—with Marlene

The British Overseas Airways Corporation created quite a sensation when they featured a bikini-clad girl basking in the surf of the West Indies. Shocking, said MPs. It had to go. The slogan of the day was an electioneering one—*Let's Go with Labour*. Front page cartoonist Jon showed a little boy pointing at the poster and saying 'Must she go with Labour, Dad?'

Jon couldn't have known that the same air firm was going to provide him with yet more material for his pocket cartoon. But they did. They picked on Marlene to show the lovely leg-room and comfort provided by the Corporation in its world travel.

The photograph they used of Marlene was a beauty. A new face was emerging, a face for the 1960s. The sharply-defined shapes of her early film career had been giving place gradually to softer lines and features.

The advertisement was primarily aimed at the States and appeared in their news magazines, *Life* and *Time* and *Newsweek*.

The corporation paid something like £70,000 on this splash 'ad' to promote their VC-10.

Some bright publicity man thought it shouldn't be restricted to the States. What was good enough for them would be good enough for Europe too. But in Frankfurt, BOAC's chief publicity man, Herr Paul Breuer, cabled the London office frantically. Don't use this advertisement in West Germany, he warned. She is very unpopular.

Herr Breuer conducted a little survey. 'The idea,' he said, 'was that we should use the picture of Miss Dietrich for our direct mail advertising in Germany. But we ran a survey as we usually do in such matters, and we found that she was unpopular.' She was remembered, he said, as wearing Allied uniform in the war, and entertaining Allied troops. Seventy-five customers had been circulated. 'We told the head of the London office that the picture would not attract German customers to fly with BOAC.'

Herr Breuer himself was courteous and dissociated himself from these unpleasant sentiments of his countrymen. 'I was thirteen when the war ended. I don't associate her with the war one way or the other.'

A journalist who took this anti-Dietrich action with a pinch of salt conducted his own survey in Bonn. He reported the results. 'Seventy per cent asked, "Is she still around?" Fifteen per cent said "I will always fly BOAC if I can have the seat next to her." Three per cent said "Marlene had trouble in the War?" One per cent said "I'd go anywhere with Marlene, but couldn't we have two tickets for a slow boat?"' A tongue-in-cheek view, perhaps, but not one indicating any special hatred for the lady.

What did Miss Dietrich say about the matter?

'Who cares?' she said disdainfully. 'Who cares about the Germans hating you when you have the affection of the British?'

She was charmingly frank when asked why she had posed for the picture. 'I was flattered. Wouldn't you be at my age? Most of the models they use in the ads have barely left school these days.'

Pressed again on her feelings towards Germany, she finally let the resentment come welling up. 'When I die, I'd like to be buried in Paris. But I'd also like to leave my heart in England. And in Germany—nothing. It's the Nazis behind all this fuss of course. There are still too many of them sitting around over there. Nothing pleases me more than their dislike of me. I could use stronger words for what I feel about them . . .'

CHAPTER THIRTY-TWO

What is Marlene?

Many famous people have tried to describe Marlene Dietrich. 'She is the most exciting and terrifying woman I have ever known,' Jean Cocteau said, after painting her. Noël Coward has commented 'Marlene is a realist and a clown.'

'Acting just happens to be my profession,' was Dietrich's reaction to this. 'I could live very well without it. I have no ambition. I've never had the message. I'm afraid that all my life I've needed a push and never done things for myself. Coward was right. I never show my clown side to the public. It doesn't go with the other thing I advertise.'

The shrewdness is typical. For Dietrich has always been conscious of her legend—of its public mask, its financial value, the responsibilities it entails—and has also quietly revealed, from time to time, that she has a sense of humour about it. The legend itself must sometimes have been difficult to preserve. For when Marlene achieved world fame as Lola-Lola in *The Blue Angel*, it was a kind of fatal woman, a beautiful aloof seductress, that stamped her immediately as a product of the twenties. This remote ideal of womanhood—languid, mysterious, a little perverse—has always seemed on the verge of being overtaken by time, and no doubt it would have been if Dietrich herself had not proved time's most persistent antagonist. Like Garbo, she is ageless; and, like Garbo, she had managed to remain an ideal while other ideals come in and out of fashion. Considered a less great actress, she has found it easier to survive in the cinema because she needs less a great part than a great personality to play. Many of her admirers say she is more of a cabaret artist, finally, than an actress—perhaps the best cabaret artist of her time, with a cunning trick of adjusting her personality every few years and striking a new note.

When Dietrich stopped working with von Sternberg, a too exquisite goddess came down to earth (somewhere near the French Riviera) and smiled—and in *Angel* she was a charming adventuress, a woman of the world, still miraculously elegant but almost approachable. A few years later she discovered her *Destry* act, and now the goddess good-naturedly disguised herself as a saloon queen, mixing with the boys in the back room, until she started off on her USO tours. Then, when she returned to the cinema, she played what was perhaps her most brilliant trick of all— she played herself. The artist at the Café de Paris seemed to have stepped straight from *Stage Fright* and *No Highway*. Her extraordinary success was due to the wheel of fashion turning full circle; many features of the twenties have been cultivated in the fifties and sixties, and Dietrich could be worshipped as an embodiment of them.

Because the dividing line between Dietrich the artist and Dietrich the woman has seemed to grow steadily more narrow, it has often been difficult to know when she is playing herself and when, simply, she is being herself. Some things are certain. She is extremely beautiful, but she has also been, at times, extremely lonely. Beauty of her kind can be its own prison, it can overawe; and though Dietrich has a legion of acquaintances, she is a woman of few close friends. For this reason her friendships with men—with Remarque, with Fairbanks, Gabin, Wilding—have always attracted excessive attention. But when a man knows her and respects her, she seems to win his wholehearted approval. 'I feel at my happiest,' Ernest Hemingway said of her, 'when I have written something I am sure is good and Marlene reads it and likes it.'

'The rumour that she is aloof,' Kenneth Tynan wrote, 'is a monstrous untruth. I think of her curled up like a sated lioness in the back seat of a car, suddenly dissolving into laughter and clutching the arm of whoever happens to be near her, and then raising her eyebrows and gnawing her lips in self-derision. . . . She has a magnificent sense of humour about herself, which means that she possesses the rarest of civilised virtues, irony. Even in her happiest embrace, the irony is there, as if she were saying through her smiles: "Imagine *us* of all people, doing the True Love bit. . . ."'

Others have disagreed. 'She takes herself as seriously as it's possible for any human being to do,' an acquaintance once pronounced. 'If an important new modern symphony were dedicated to Marlene Dietrich, she wouldn't accept the dedication unless she had taken steps to make sure it was a *good* symphony.'

A Hollywood director who made a film with her calls her 'a rather old-fashioned girl. Everything about her seems somewhat quaint and Germanic—including her Wagnerian self-love. There is always a sort of fascination about people who manage to exist beyond the period in which they were appropriate symbols—a little like the Walt Disney animals who run off a cliff and walk on air for a few moments before they discover it.'

'I dislike intrusion of any sort—especially intrusion on my private life,' Dietrich has said. 'I believe in Fate, not in Luck. And I imagine Fate has other things in store for me than the gift of avoiding intruders. My work is my interest in life, apart from my family.' If she were not a film star, she would like to be a cameraman. But being a film star, she accepted her duties entirely. 'There is really no time when I dislike being in the public gaze— public life for a film star is as much of a duty as making a film. I have no hobbies—I have no time for anything but my work.'

She recognises the need for discipline in maintaining health and beauty. 'Gluttony is the cause of most avoidable illnesses.' On a typical day she will start with an orange for breakfast, probably lunch off a vegetable salad, and eat a steak for dinner.

The Dietrich approach to food perplexes most people. She's a good cook, and insists she likes simple, home cooking. But for herself?

Michael Wilding watched her with fascination. 'She eats chocolate, bread, potatoes. Marlene, I think, sincerely believes that her body is just a kind of container like a cellophane wrapper and that beauty comes from the inside. A thing of the mind. So she can go all night without sleep. Hours without food.'

She herself has gone on record as saying things like 'Give me good plain English food. Give me some suet pudding and I'll be happy.'

Not only English food, though. 'I like cooking Russian, French, and Austrian peasant dishes. I am not so keen on elegant cooking or what you might call "La Cuisine Française" with lots of wine sauces.' This doesn't stop her cooking them. She startled Michael Wilding when she once discovered him in a mournful state, by taking his ration book and striding out into the butcher's with a friend, taking her place at the end of a queue along with the regular customers. She came back with kidneys, quite an achievement in those days of rationing. 'She served them in a flaming brandy sauce,' said Michael Wilding. 'They were sensational. I didn't know that kidneys could taste or look like that.'

While they were filming Stanley Kramer's *Judgment at Nuremberg* there was a scene where they all had to eat apfelstrudel. 'Listen,' she said. 'If we're going to have apfelstrudel, it's going to be the best apfelstrudel. And nobody makes apfelstrudel like Dietrich.'

Kramer was impressed when she arrived next day with the apfelstrudel. 'The best goddammed apfelstrudel you ever saw,' he said.

A speciality of hers is *Pot au Feu*, the French peasant way of simmering meat with vegetables which gives you a delicious broth, as well as meat and vegetables for the course to follow. She takes the trouble to cook for people who care. If they don't, then she won't. And they never know what they are missing.

The first time Nancy Spain met her, she was surprised to find that the artist was content to eat an evening meal of 'coagulated steak and French fried potatoes' out of a paper bag. For breakfast Miss Dietrich ate boiled eggs, and 'dropped butter in the broken tops like a child,' Miss Spain reported. 'She doesn't notice what she eats and drinks.' But later Miss Spain revised her opinion, and included a Dietrich recipe for fish in a celebrity cookery book.

On one occasion at a New York party a guest was talking about food and mentioned a fashionable new gimmick, a submarine sandwich, made of a French loaf three feet long, packed with 17 slices of ham, 15 slices of garlic sausage, 12 slices of smoked Italian ham, 24 slices of provolone cheese, 20 slices of raw smoked beef, chopped green peppers, tomatoes, pickles, and olive oil and tarragon vinegar dressing. The whole 'submarine' weighed 2½ lb. She asked politely where it could be bought. Then she left the party.

It was learned later that she had taken a taxi straight to a shop on the New York waterfront which was selling 'submarines', and took one home to provide dinner for herself, her daughter and son-in-law.

Bread. Potatoes. Chocolate. How does she manage to keep so slim?

She once advanced a theory herself, which may explain it to some. 'One meal a day and *gebauchgymnastik*,' she said to a mystified questioner. Then she explained that *gebauchgymnastik* was internal exercise of the stomach. You think of various muscles, she said, and flex them and unflex them at will. You can do it whether you're walking, sitting, or even reclining.

There are many anecdotes that illustrate the sometimes conflicting traits of her character—her extreme business acumen and her superstition (astrology), her generosity and her solitude, her humour and her sometimes surprising lack of it. (Discussing Hitler after the war, she said: 'I sometimes wonder if I just might have been the one person in the world who could have prevented the war and saved millions of lives. It troubles me a lot and I'll never stop worrying about it.') Hollywood well remembers the 1950 Academy Award Dinner, when Marlene had been invited to present the Foreign Award. The honour necessitated a brief trip across the stage of Los Angeles' Pantages Theatre and a short, polite speech—that was all. Dietrich first checked the colour scheme of the setting in which the ceremony was to be held; it was red, white and blue. She then cast around and learned from friends the colours that other Hollywood stars had chosen to wear, and was told that fluffy pinks, whites and greys would predominate. 'Then Momma is going to wear black,' she said.

There is often a dryness in the way she likes to perpetuate her own legend. She once remarked that the greatest gift a man could possess was tact, and told how she once said to the cameraman for *The Garden of Allah*: 'When you were filming *The Garden of Allah*, you made me look gorgeous. Why aren't these shots so good?' The cameraman answered: 'Well, Marlene, I'm eight years older now.' That, she considered, was the epitome of tact.

There is also her famous 'Funeral Story', which she often tells at parties. She explains that when she dies, only the men who have known her well will be permitted to attend her funeral. Her husband, Rudolph, equipped with a list, will be posted at the door to keep out gate-crashers—the many men who have falsely claimed to have been her friend. Then Dietrich caricatures the men who will be admitted: a list that grows longer as time goes by. Douglas Fairbanks Jnr will turn up in full dress naval uniform, bearing a wreath from the Queen of England; Jean Gabin will be leaning against the church door, a cigarette dangling from his lips, disdaining to join the other mourners; Remarque, with characteristic vagueness, will be at the wrong church, mourning the wrong funeral . . .

Marlene now lives in a fashionable four-roomed apartment in New York. It has what somebody described as 'a cluttered elegance'. She has many books; the works of Shakespeare, Shelley, Tolstoy, Goethe, Dostoievsky, William James and Ernest Hemingway are on her shelves. A Sheraton table in her living-room proudly mounts her prized autographed picture of Hemingway—'To Marlene, if she still loves me or if she doesn't—Papa.' On the walls of her apartment hang most of her personal fortune, for she has invested soundly in pictures by Chagall, Delacroix, Utrillo—'Maurice's streets and snows'—Picasso, Corot and Cézanne. One of her favourite pictures is Picasso's *The Absinthe Drinker*. 'I own it, so I can look at it as much as I like.' Sometimes she gives a small party for intimate friends, such as Tallulah Bankhead, Eva Gabor, Judy Garland, Hildegarde Neff. Sometimes she contemplates her personal finances, which are complicated like those of most high-earning artists, many of whom believe that if you earn a thousand pounds you own a thousand pounds.

She is often visited by her daughter and son-in-law and their children. And Rudolph Sieber, her husband, who has remained in the background of her life for nearly thirty years, spends much of his time at the apartment when he is in New York.

For one who has bathed so long in the public spotlight her private life is relatively secluded. She still makes world tours, is ever planning, is still finding new worlds to conquer. But at home, she says, 'It is my private life which no one knows anything about, nor ever will. It needs more than half my time if it is to be a success.'

She says she has no more ambitions, but the possibility of new media is always intriguing to her. She played on sound radio in a BBC play, *The Child*, very successfully. And though she has said she did not want to appear on television, BBC 2 managed to persuade Swedish television to let them screen a Dietrich performance from a Swedish restaurant. Once she said she would have liked to act in a Christopher Fry play, *The Dark is Light Enough*. She occasionally makes an LP record. Each one goes on selling with almost monotonous regularity.

Dietrich by her Friends

What is Marlene? Pause and consider for a moment. What she is in her films. What she is on the stage. What she is in interviews. What she is in newspapers. What she is to her friends. Take a final look at some of the jig-saw pieces provided by her friends and consider . . .

Peter Brook, theatre producer: 'When I was producing *House of Flowers* in the United States, Marlene would come backstage every night, acting as honorary wardrobe mistress. The actresses were all screaming for her to sew on buttons.'

Harold Arlen, songwriter: 'When I got my bug they thought I was going to die. Marlene was at the hospital every day with flowers and fruit and her present of eternal youth. She saw me through. She had the doctors rushing about.'

Mischa Spoliansky, who once pulled Marlene's leg, when the star had invited the penicillin discoverer, Fleming, to dinner: 'Marlene nearly went mad trying to find out what his favourite food was. I said it was haggis. She didn't know what that was, much less how to cook it. If you are no good at haggis, I told her, he is very fond of grouse. One thing Marlene doesn't like to cook is roasts. She likes to taste everything as it goes along. . . .'

The New York drama critic who took her to a play: 'She wouldn't tell me what she thought of the play. She wouldn't want anyone to think she was affecting my critical judgment.'

Oliver Messel, the painter and stage designer: 'When I went to the States to do the sets for *Rashomon*, the stage play, she was a great friend. When I got to my flat she had already set up all the tables and materials I would need for my work. Every item was exactly right. She was also very helpful over lighting, and she made some brilliant suggestions on the production. She ought to be a producer.'

Stanley Kramer, the film producer: 'Dietrich—well, she will always be Dietrich. Fastidious to a degree and a genius at spending your money.'

Bessie Braddock: 'She's superb.'

Richard Burton: 'I adore her—the most beautiful woman I've ever met. In a curious way like a skeleton risen from the grave, face bones barely covered with make-up. Arise, oh beautiful bones. Beautiful and extraordinary. Besides, she cooks well.'

Pastovsky, the Russian writer: 'If I had not yet written *The Telegram* [which she admired] I would write it for you now. I will write a story for you.'

Lord Harewood, Edinburgh Festival organiser, when asked about her return visit: 'The arrangement is more mutual than you might think.'

Harold Hobson, theatre critic: 'At her best she is better than Chevalier because more tender in feeling; better even than Piaf, whose thrilling voice was uncomfortably enormous for the sorrows she used to sing about so memorably. . . . Miss Dietrich shows us the height and depth of love by catching it with an infallible precision in the very moment of its defeat.'

'Everything there is to say about me has been said,' she considers. 'I'm not much, nothing spectacular. A director once said to me when I was making a picture—"Come now, give me *Marlene* . . ."

'"What is Marlene?" I asked him. "I do not know . . ."'

The Films of Marlene Dietrich made in Germany and France

DIE TRAGODIE DER LIEBE   Germany, 1923

Directed by Joe May

Starred Emil Jannings as a brutal Parisian prize-fighter in a below-stairs melodrama. He kills a butler, his rival for the affections of a pretty chambermaid, who betrays him to the gendarmes. Dietrich appears briefly as a judge's ladyfriend who wants to attend the trial. A print of this film is in the collection of George Eastman House.

THE GREAT BARITONE   Germany, 1924

Cast:
Albert Basserman
Marlene Dietrich

MANON LESCAUT   Germany, 1926   9 *reels*

Prod Co:	UFA	*Cast:*
Director:	Arthur Robison	Lys de Putti
Author:	Based on the novel by	Vladimir Gaidavov
	Abbé Prévost and the	Eduard Rothausser
	opera by Jules Massenet	Fritz Greiner
		Marlene Dietrich
Photography:	Theodor Sparkuhl	Frida Richard
Sets:	Paul Leni	Theodor Loos
		Siegfried Arno
		Hubert von Meyerlinck

The love story of Manon and the Chevalier de Grieux. Dietrich's minor role is that of the woman who replaces Manon in prison.

WENN EIN WEIB DEN WEG VERHÄRT   *Vienna, 1926*

Prod Co: Sascha Films   *Cast:*
Director: Gustave Ucicky   Marlene Dietrich

GEFAHREN DER BRAUTZEIT   *Germany, 1926*

Prod Co: Hegewald Films   *Cast:*
Director: Fred Sauer   Elsa Tamary
                                       Willy Forst
                                       Marlene Dietrich
                                       Ernst Stahl-Nachbauer

SEIN GRÖSSTER BLUFF   *Germany, 1927   10 reels*

Prod Co: Nero Films   *Cast:*
Director: Harry Piel   Harry Piel
Script: Henrick Galeen   Lotte Lorring
Photography: Muschner and Wolff   Marlene Dietrich

ICH KÜSSE IHRE HAND, MADAME   *Germany, 1929*

English title: *I Kiss your Little Hand, Madam*

Prod Co: Super Films   *Cast:*
Director: Robert Lind   Harry Liedtke
Script: Rolf E Vanloo   Pierre de Guingand
Photography: Fritz Brunn, Carl Drews,   Karl Huszar-Puffy
                 Gotthard Wolff   Marlene Dietrich

PRINZESS IN OLALA   *Germany, 1928–9*

English title: *The Art of Love*

Prod Co: Super Films   *Cast:*
Director: Robert Lind   Marlene Dietrich
Photography: Willy Goldberger   Ileena Meery
                                        Walter Rilla
                                        Carmen Boni
                                        George Alexander

Based on popular operetta by Frank Schultz, it provided Dietrich
with her first starring role.

DIE FRAU NACH DER MAN SICH SEHNT   *Germany, 1929*

English title: *Three Loves*

Prod Co:	Terra Films	*Cast:*
Director:	Kurt Bernhardt	Marlene Dietrich
		Uno Henning
		Fritz Kortner

DAS SCHIFF DER VERLORENEN MENSCHEN
Germany, 1929   7 reels

French title: *Le Navire des Hommes Perdus*

Producer:	Max Glass	*Cast:*
Director:	Maurice Tourneur	Marlene Dietrich
Author:	From a novel by Franzos	Fritz Kortner
	Kerzemen	Gaston Modot
Photography:	Nikolaus Farkas	Boris de Fast

LIEBESNÄCHTE   *Germany, 1929   6 reels*

Prod Co:	Strauss Films	*Cast:*
Director:	Fred Sauer	Lotte Lorring
Script:	Walter Wasserman,	Willy Först
	Walter Schlee	Ernst Stahl-Nachbauer
Photography:	L Schaffer	Marlene Dietrich

DER BLAUE ENGEL   *Germany, 1930*

English title: *The Blue Angel*

Prod Co:	UFA	*Cast:*
Director:	Josef von Sternberg	Emil Jannings
Author:	Heinrich Mann,	Marlene Dietrich
	Professor Unrath	Hans Albers
Script:	Robert Liebmann	Kurt Gerron
	from the adaptation by	Rosa Valetti
	Karl Zuckmayer and	Hans Roth
	Karl Vollmoller	Eduard von Winterstein
Photography:	Gunther Rittau,	Rolf Muller
	Hans Schneeberger	Rolant Varno
Music:	Friedrich Hollander	Carl Balhaus
		Reinhold Bernt

MARTIN ROUMAGNAC

Prod Co:	Alcina
Producer:	Marc Le Pelletier
Director:	Georges Lacombe
Author:	Pierre-Rene Wolf
Photography:	Robert Hubert
Script:	Georges Lacombe
Art Director:	Georges Wakhevitch
Music:	Marcel Mirouze

Cast:
Marlene Dietrich
Jean Gabin
Margo Lion
Jean D'Yd
Marcel Herrand

The Films of Marlene Dietrich made in the United States and Britain

MOROCCO

USA, 1930

Prod Co:	Paramount
Director:	Josef von Sternberg
Author:	Benno Vigny from *Amy Jolly*
Script:	Jules Furthman
Photography:	Lee Garmes
Editor:	Sam Winston

Cast:
Marlene Dietrich
Gary Cooper
Adolphe Menjou
Ulrich Haput
Juliette Compton
Francis MacDonald

DISHONOURED

USA, 1931

Prod Co:	Paramount
Director:	Josef von Sternberg
Author:	Josef von Sternberg
Script:	Daniel N Rubin
Photography:	Lee Garmes
Sound:	Harry D Mills

Cast:
Marlene Dietrich
Victor McLaglen
Lew Cody
Warner Oland
Gustav von Seyffertitz
Barry Norton

SHANGHAI EXPRESS

USA, 1932

Prod Co:	Paramount
Director:	Josef von Sternberg
Author:	Harry Hervey
Script:	Jules Furthman
Photography:	Lee Garmes

Cast:
Marlene Dietrich
Clive Brook
Anna May Wong
Warner Oland
Eugene Pallette

BLONDE VENUS

USA, 1932

Prod Co:	Paramount
Director:	Josef von Sternberg
Script:	Jules Furthman, S K Lauren
Photography:	Bert Glennon
Art Director:	Wiard Ihnen
Songs:	*Hot Voodoo* and *You Little So-and-So* by Sam Coslow and Ralph Rainger
	I Couldn't Be Annoyed by Leo Robin and Dick Whiting

Cast:
Marlene Dietrich
Herbert Marshall
Cary Grant
Dickie Moore
Gene Morgan
Rita La Roy

SONG OF SONGS

USA, 1933

Prod Co:	Paramount
Director:	Rouben Mamoulian
Author:	Hermann Sudermann
Script:	Leo Birinski, Samuel Hoffenstein
Photography:	Victor Milner

Cast:
Marlene Dietrich
Brian Aherne
Lionel Atwill
Alison Skipworth

THE SCARLET EMPRESS

USA, 1933

Prod Co:	Paramount
Director:	Josef von Sternberg
Script:	Manuel Komroff
Photography:	Bert Glennon
Art Director:	Hans Dreier
Costumes:	Travis Banton
Music:	Based on Tschaikowsky and Mendelssohn, arranged by John M Leipold, W Frank Harding

Cast:
Marlene Dietrich
John Lodge
Sam Jaffe
C Aubrey Smith
Louise Dresser
Maria Sieber
Gavin Gordon

THE DEVIL IS A WOMAN

Prod Co: Paramount
Director: Josef von Sternberg
Author: Pierre Louys: *The Woman and the puppet*
Script: John Dos Passos
Photography: Josef von Sternberg
Editor: Sam Winston
Music and Lyrics: Ralph Rainger, Leo Robin

Cast:
Marlene Dietrich
Lionel Atwill
Cesar Romero
Edward Everett Horton
Alison Skipworth

DESIRE

Prod Co: Paramount
Producer: Ernst Lubitsch
Director: Frank Borzage
Authors: Hans Szekeley, R A Stemmle
Script: Edwin Justus Mayer, Waldemar Young, Samuel Hoffenstein
Photography: Charles Lang
Editor: William Shea
Music and Lyrics: Frederick Hollander, Leo Robin

Cast:
Marlene Dietrich
Gary Cooper
John Halliday
Akim Tamiroff
Alan Mowbray

THE GARDEN OF ALLAH

Prod Co: Selznick International
Director: Richard Boleslawski
Author: Robert Hitchens
Script: Willis Goldbeck, W P Lipscomb, Lyn Riggs
Photography: W Howard Green
Editor: Hal C Kern
Music: Max Steiner

Cast:
Marlene Dietrich
Charles Boyer
Tilly Losch
Basil Rathbone
Joseph Schildkraut
John Carradine

KNIGHT WITHOUT ARMOUR
Britain, 1937

Prod Co:	London Films
Director:	Jacques Feyder
Producer:	Alexander Korda
Author:	James Hilton
Script:	Frances Marion
Photography:	Jack Cardiff
Editor:	Francis Lyon

Cast:
Marlene Dietrich
Robert Donat
Herbert Lomas
Austin Trevor
John Clements
David Tree
Basil Gill

ANGEL
USA, 1937

Prod Co:	Paramount
Director:	Ernst Lubitsch
Producer:	Ernst Lubitsch
Author:	Melchior Lengyl
Script:	Samson Raphaelson
Art Directors:	Hans Dreier, Robert Usher
Musical Director:	Boris Morros
Music and Lyrics:	Frederick Hollander, Leo Robin
Photography:	Charles Lang
Editor:	William Shea

Cast:
Marlene Dietrich
Herbert Marshall
Melvyn Douglas
Edward Everett Horton
Laura Hope Crews

DESTRY RIDES AGAIN
USA, 1939

Prod Co:	Universal
Director:	George Marshall
Producer:	Joseph Pasternak
Author:	Max Brand
Script:	Felix Jackson, Gertrude Purcell, Henry Myers
Photography:	Hal Mohr
Editor:	Milton Carruth

Cast:
James Stewart
Charles Winninger
Brian Donlevy
Marlene Dietrich
Una Merkel
Irene Hervey
Jack Carson
Warren Hymer
Allen Jenkins

SEVEN SINNERS

USA, *1940*

Prod Co: Universal
Director: Tay Garnett
Producer: Joe Pasternak
Authors: Ladislaus Fodor,
Laslo Vadnai
Script: John Meehan,
Harry Tugend
Photography: Rudolph Mate
Editor: Ted Kent

Cast:
Marlene Dietrich
John Wayne
Albert Dekker
Broderick Crawford
Anna Lee
Mischa Auer
Billy Gilbert
Oscar Homolka

THE FLAME OF NEW ORLEANS

USA, *1941*

Prod Co: Universal
Director: René Clair
Script: Harry Fraser
Producer: Joe Pasternak
Photography: Rudolph Mate
Editor: Frank Gross

Cast:
Marlene Dietrich
Roland Young
Bruce Cabot

MANPOWER

USA, *1941*

Prod Co: Warner
Director: Raoul Walsh
Script: Richard Macauley,
Jerry Wald

Cast:
Marlene Dietrich
Edward G Robinson
George Raft

THE LADY IS WILLING

USA, *1942*

Prod Co: Columbia
Director: Mitchell Leisen
Script: James Edward Grant,
Albert McCleery
Author: James Edward Grant
Photography: Ted Tetzlaff
Editor: Eda Warren
Art Director: Lionel Banks

Cast:
Marlene Dietrich
Fred MacMurray
Aline MacMahon
Stanley Ridges
Ruth Ford
Sterling Holloway

THE SPOILERS

USA, 1942

Prod Co: Universal
Producer: Frank Lloyd
Director: Ray Enright
Author: Rex Beach
Script: Lawrence Hazard,
Tom Reed
Art Director: Jack Otterson
Photography: Milton Krasner
Editor: Clarence Kolster

Cast:
Marlene Dietrich
Randolph Scott
John Wayne
Margaret Lindsay
Harry Carey
Richard Barthelmess
George Cleveland

PITTSBURGH

USA, 1942

Prod Co: Universal
Director: Lewis Seiler
Producer: Robert Fellows
Author: George Olsen,
Tom Reed
Script: Kenneth Gamet,
Tom Reed
Photography: Robert DeGrasse
Editor: Paul Landers
Art Director: Jack Otterson
Music: Charles Previn

Cast:
Marlene Dietrich
John Wayne
Randolph Scott
Frank Craven
Louise Allbritton
Thomas Gomez
Ludwig Stossel

FOLLOW THE BOYS

USA, 1944

Prod Co: Universal
Producer: Charles K Feldman
Director: Edward Sutherland
Script: Lou Breslow,
Gertrude Purcell
Photography: David Abel
Art Directors: John G Goodman,
Harold H MacArthur
*Dance
Director:* George Hale
Music: Leigh Harline

Cast:
Marlene Dietrich
George Raft
Vera Zorina
Orson Welles
W C Fields
Dinah Shore

KISMET

		Cast:
Prod Co:	MGM	Marlene Dietrich
Producer:	Everett Riskin	Ronald Colman
Director:	William Dieterle	James Craig
Author:	Edward Knoblock	Edward Arnold
Script:	John Meehan	Hugh Herbert
Photography:	Charles Rosher	Joy Ann Page
Editor:	Ben Lewis	Florence Bates
Music:	Herbert Stothart	Harry Davenport
Songs:	Harold Arlen,	
	E Y Harburg	
Art Directors:	Cedric Gibbons,	
	Daniel B Cathcart	

GOLDEN EARRINGS

		Cast:
Prod Co:	Paramount	Marlene Dietrich
Producer:	Harry Tugend	Ray Milland
Director:	Mitchell Leisen	Murvyn Vye
Script:	Abraham Polonsky,	
	Frank Butler,	
	Helen Deutsch	
Photography:	Daniel L Fapp	
Editor:	Alma McCrorie	
Music:	Victor Young	
Art Director:	Hans Dreier	

A FOREIGN AFFAIR

		Cast:
Prod Co:	Paramount	Marlene Dietrich
Producer:	Charles Brackett	Jean Arthur
Director:	Billy Wilder	John Lund
Author:	David Shaw	Millard Mitchell
Script:	Charles Brackett,	
	Billy Wilder,	
	Richard L Breen	
Photography:	Charles B Lang Jr	
Editor:	Deane Harrison	
Music:	Frederick Hollander	

STAGE FRIGHT

Britain, 1950

Prod Co:	Warner
Producer:	Alfred Hitchcock
Director:	Alfred Hitchcock
Author:	Selwyn Jepson, *Man Running*
Script:	Whitfield Cook
Photography:	Wilkie Cooper
Editor:	Edward Jarvis
Art Director:	Terence Verity
Music:	Leighton Lucas
Miss Dietrich's Wardrobe:	Christian Dior
Musical Director:	Louis Levy
Song:	*I'm the Laziest Gal in Town* by Cole Porter

Cast:
Marlene Dietrich
Jane Wyman
Richard Todd
Michael Wilding
Alastair Sim
Kay Walsh
Sybil Thorndike
André Morell

NO HIGHWAY

Britain, 1951

Prod Co:	20th Century Fox
Producer:	Louis D Lighton
Director:	Henry Koster
Author:	Nevil Shute
Script:	R C Sherriff, Oscar Millard, Alec Coppel
Photography:	Georges Ferinal
Editor:	Manuel de Campo
Art Director:	C P Norman

Cast:
Marlene Dietrich
James Stewart
Glynis Johns
Jack Hawkins
Ronald Squire
Janette Scott

RANCHO NOTORIOUS

USA, 1952

Prod Co:	RKO
Producer:	Howard Welsch
Director:	Fritz Lang
Author:	Sylvia Richards
Script:	Daniel Taradash
Photography:	Hal Mohr
Editor:	Otto Ludwig

Cast:
Marlene Dietrich
Arthur Kennedy
Mel Ferrer
Gloria Henry
Lloyd Gough

45 I

AROUND THE WORLD IN 80 DAYS — USA, *1956*

Prod Co:	Michael Todd Productions	
Producer:	Michael Todd	
Director:	Michael Anderson	
Assistant Producer:	William Cameron Menzies	
Screenplay:	James Poe, S J Perelman, John Farrow	
Author:	Based on a novel by Jules Verne	
Music:	Victor Young	
Costumes:	Miles White	
Choreography:	Paul Godkin	
Art Directors:	James Sullivan, Ken Adams	
Photography:	Lionel Lindon	
Location Director:	Kevin McClory	

Cast:
Marlene Dietrich
David Niven
Cantinflas
Robert Newton
Shirley MacLaine
Charles Boyer
Sir John Gielgud
John Mills
Joe E Brown
Hermione Gingold
Robert Morley
Martine Carol
José Greco
Alan Mowbray
John Carradine
Sir Cedric Hardwicke
Ed Murrow
Charles Coburn
Trevor Howard
Jack Oakie
Ronald Colman
Glynis Johns
George Raft
Melville Cooper
Buster Keaton
Gilbert Roland
Noël Coward
Evelyn Keyes
Cesar Romero
Finlay Currie
Beatrice Lillie
Frank Sinatra
Reginald Denny
Peter Lorre
Red Skelton
Andy Devine

Edmund Lowe
Ronald Squire
Col Tim McCoy
Basil Sydney
Luis Dominguin
Victor McLaglen
Richard Wattis
Fernandel
A E Matthews
Harcourt Williams
Walter Fitzgerald
Mike Mazurki

THE MONTE CARLO STORY

USA|*Italy*|*France*, 1956

Prod Co:	Titanus
Producer:	Marcello Girosi
Director:	Samuel Taylor
Screenplay:	Samuel Taylor
Photography:	Giuseppe Rotunno
Art Director:	Gastoni Medin
Original Story:	Marcello Girosi, Dino Risi

Cast:
Marlene Dietrich
Vittorio de Sica
Arthur O'Connell
Natalie Trundy
Jane Rose
Clelia Matania
Alberto Rabagliati
Mischa Auer
Renato Rascel
Carlo Rizzo
Trueman Smith
Mimo Billi
Marco Tulli
Guido Martufi
Jean Combal
Vera Garretto
Yannick Geffroy
Betty Philippsen
Frank Colson
Serge Fliegers
Frank Elliott
Betty Carter
Gerlaine Fournier
Simonemarie Rose
Clara Beck

WITNESS FOR THE PROSECUTION   USA, 1957

Prod Co:	Arthur Hornblower Productions	*Cast:*
Producer:	Arthur Hornblower Jnr	Marlene Dietrich
Director:	Billy Wilder	Tyrone Power
Screenplay:	Billy Wilder and Harry Kurnitz	Charles Laughton
Adaptation:	Larry Marcus	Elsa Lanchester
Stage Play:	Agatha Christie	John Williams
Photography:	Russell Harlan	Henry Daniell
assisted by:	Emmett Emerson	Ian Wolfe
Miss Dietrich's		Una O'Connor
Costumes:	Edith Head	Torin Thatcher
Film Editor:	Daniel Mandell	Frances Compton
Art Director:	Alexandre Trauner	Norma Varden
Musical score:	Matty Malneck	Philip Tonge
Musical Ar-		Ruta Lee
rangements:	Leonid Raab	Molly Roden
Conductor:	Ernest Gold	Ottola Nesmith
Song:	*I May Never Go Home Anymore* by Ralph Arthur Roberts and Jack Brooks	Marjorie Eaton

Cast:
Marlene Dietrich
Tyrone Power
Charles Laughton
Elsa Lanchester
John Williams
Henry Daniell
Ian Wolfe
Una O'Connor
Torin Thatcher
Frances Compton
Norma Varden
Philip Tonge
Ruta Lee
Molly Roden
Ottola Nesmith
Marjorie Eaton

TOUCH OF EVIL   USA, 1958

Prod Co:	Universal International	*Cast:*
Producer:	Albert Zugsmith	Charlton Heston
Director:	Orson Welles	Janet Leigh
Cameraman:	Russell Metty	Orson Welles
Film Editors:	Virgil Vogel and Aaron Stell	Joseph Calleia
Art Directors:	Alexander Golitzen and Robert Clatworthy	Akim Tamiroff
Music:	Henry Mancini	Marlene Dietrich (guest star)

JUDGMENT AT NUREMBERG   USA, 1961

Prod Co:	Roxlom
Producer and	
Director:	Stanley Kramer
Associate	
Producer:	Philip Langner
Screenplay:	Abbey Mann
Camera:	Ernest Laszlo
Editor:	Fred Knudtson
Music:	Ernest Gold
Assistant to	
Director:	Ivan Volkman
Production	
Designer:	Rudolph Sternad
Wardrobe:	Joe King
Property	
Master:	Art Cole
Production	
Manager:	Clem Beauchamp

Cast:
Marlene Dietrich
Spencer Tracy
Burt Lancaster
Richard Widmark
Maximilian Schell
Judy Garland
Montgomery Clift
William Shatner
Ed Binns
Kenneth Mackenna
Werner Klemperer
Alan Baxter
Torben Meyer
Ray Teal
Martin Brandt
Virginia Christine
Ben Wright
Joseph Bernard
John Wengraf
Karl Swenson
Howard Caine
Otto Waldis
Olga Fabian
Sheila Bromley
Bernard Kates
Jana Taylor
Paul Busch

BLACK FOX   USA, 1962

Prod Co:	Image Productions
Producer and	
Director:	Louis Clyde Stoumen

Narration by Marlene Dietrich